TEACHING
Children's
Literature

Linda Cox Story

Kendall Hunt
publishing company

Cover photos courtesy of Linda Cox Story.

www.kendallhunt.com
Send all inquiries to:
4050 Westmark Drive
Dubuque, IA 52004-1840

Copyright © 2018 by Kendall Hunt Publishing Company

ISBN: 978-1-5249-7121-2

Published in the United States of America

Contents

Introduction

"Books are the carriers of civilization. Without books, history is silent, literature dumb, science crippled, thought and speculation at a standstill."—Barbara Tuchman

Most elementary and middle school language arts teachers did not major in literature in college; they majored in education. In many cases, prospective language arts teachers have no greater knowledge base of literature than of any other core subject. This means that if they are to be effective language arts teachers, they probably need to fortify their content knowledge. This text is intended for elementary and middle school teacher candidates who need to do just that.

Arguably, there is no more important subject area than language arts. Language arts is generally described as reading, writing, and speaking, although listening is an important element as well. Language arts is the foundation of understanding all other content. For example, an article by Sarah D. Sparks in *Education Week* in 2011 cited a study released by the American Education Research Association indicating that a student who does not read at grade level by grade three is four times less likely to graduate on time than a student who reads at grade level (Sparks 2011). Such studies abound in professional literature. Children who learn to enjoy books become better readers, so it follows that cultivating a love of reading in a child is one of the most important things a teacher can do.

In most states, teacher candidates must pass licensing examinations that require demonstration of a foundational knowledge in content areas. The *Praxis* prelicensing examination for elementary teachers is the *Elementary Education: Multiple Subjects Test, 5001*. Within the multiple subjects test is the subtest, 5002, *Reading and Language Arts*. Ninety (90) minutes are allowed for this subtest on the *Praxis* licensing examination. Mathematics, social studies, and science are allotted sixty-five (65), fifty (50), and fifty (50) minutes, respectively (ETS). From the amount of time devoted to the *Reading and Language Arts Subtest* alone, we can deduce the importance of language arts skills for young children. It follows that teachers must be well equipped to facilitate children in their growth in these important competencies.

Readers will find this text to be slightly different from many that cover the topic of children's literature. The difference is that this text is designed to build a knowledge base from which teachers will draw when they begin teaching and will also assist them as they prepare for licensing examinations. For example: There is a grammar review at the conclusion of the first seven chapters—unusual for a children's literature text. There are several reasons for the inclusion of the grammar reviews:

1. Although most college students exhibit adequate writing skills, many have forgotten the fundamentals of grammar, such as the function of various parts of speech in a sentence, that they learned while they were P–12 students. You can't teach it if you don't know it.

2. Language arts teachers must be well versed in the foundations of writing, including grammar. It is absolutely necessary that teachers should be proficient in the content that they teach.

3. Several basic grammar questions may appear on Praxis subtest 5002, and the grammar reviews can help with that.

The goal of this text is to assist prospective teachers in becoming effective language arts teachers. In order for teacher candidates to become effective teachers of language arts, this text will assist teacher candidates in meeting the following objectives:

1. Build a knowledge base of the history, elements, and instructional uses of literature.

2. Build a knowledge base of the vast repertoire of literature for children and resources for teaching.

3. Understand the use of children's books to promote growth in cognition, social skills, and learning across the curriculum.

4. Understand the competencies and skills required in the literature sections of the *Praxis Elementary Education Reading and Language Arts Subtest 5002*. Throughout the text, the reader will find some words typed in **bold,** which the author believes are important for purposes of licensing examinations.

Chapter 1

Language Acquisition and Development in Children

Alignments

▶ International Literacy Association: Standard 1
▶ InTASC, Standards: 1.d, 1.e, 2.a, 2.e
▶ ETS, Praxis Exam: 5002 b *Test Specifications*
▶ WIDA (World Class Instructional Design and Assessment): Standard 1
▶ NCTE/CAEP: Standard 1.1, 2.2, 3.2

Framework

The American Speech–Language–Hearing Association (ASHA) defines language as "the words we use and how we use them to share ideas and get what we want." Among all animals, humans alone possess the ability to learn and use complex language. The English language is capable of elaborate and detailed expression. Consider practically any line from any of Shakespeare's plays. For example, from Henry IV, Part II, Act 3, Scene 1: "Uneasy lies the head that wears a crown." In this one economical line, Shakespeare conveys meaning that would require a minimum of a paragraph to explain in prose; and yet, the reader fully understands the complexity of the author's meaning. The power of language is miraculous.

Acquisition Theories

Literacy skills are identified as *listening, speaking, reading,* and *writing*. The idea that **reading and writing develop simultaneously** and that children develop preliteracy skills prior to entering school where they will learn conventional literacy is called **emergent literacy**. One of the earliest to use this term was **Marie Clay** in her doctoral dissertation in 1966. Clay's theory and those of subsequent researchers has served as an impetus for focusing on teaching and developing oral language skills at home and in preschools. There is a focus on **social interaction** in the teaching of these skills. In other words, children should be nurtured and supported by adults in the development of all language skills. It should be noted that the term "**emergent**" is a common one in education and is often used to refer to any set of developing skills. In literacy, it refers to the observation that emergence is a **continuum that flows from one stage to another** without defined beginning and ending points.

This chapter will focus on the acquisition of speaking, reading, and writing competencies. Each component of literacy has certain characteristic developmental milestones. How is it possible for human beings to understand and use language? What are the cognitive mechanisms that allow us to learn this unique skill? There is no clear way to account for this ability, but there are four major theories that attempt to describe *how* the cognitive process of language acquisition occurs:

1. **Behaviorist/Learning Perspective Theory**

   Probably, the best-known proponent of the behaviorist theory of language acquisition is **Benjamin Frederic Skinner** (1904–1990). Skinner is considered by scholars to be a pioneer in the field of behavioral psychology, and his theories are studied in basic psychology and education methodology courses across the country.

   Skinner is particularly well known for his theory of **operant conditioning**, wherein he proposed that virtually, all human behavior is the result of a stimulus–response mechanism within the brain. In a nutshell, Skinner posited that behaviors, which are met with either a positive stimulus or the removal of negative stimulus are likely to increase. Both the provision of a positive stimulus and the removal of a negative one were termed by Skinner as **positive reinforcement**. Likewise, behaviors that are met with what the organism (human, for our purposes) perceives as punishment are likely to decrease. *Figure 1.1* provides a simplification of Skinner's theory in that Skinner considered many other mitigating factors such as the motivation of the organism, the strength of stimuli, and so forth.

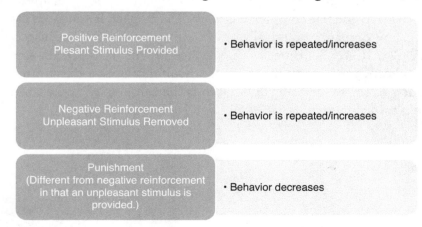

Figure 1. Skinner's Theory of Operant Conditioning.

Skinner's theory of language acquisition and development aligns with his general thinking related to the theory of operant conditioning. Skinner believed that children develop language as a result of stimuli; in other words, they develop language because they *need* to develop it in order to get what they want and need. As a child imitates the language of the parents and grows more proficient in that imitation, the child is rewarded with either positive stimuli or the removal of negative stimuli, thus increasing the development of language (McLeod).

2. **Nativist or Innatist** Theory (Sometimes called the learning approach; although, the term can be misleading because all theories of language acquisition are language learning approaches.)

   Noam Chomsky (born 1928) is considered the progenitor of the nativist view of language acquisition. Essentially, Chomsky holds that the acquisition of language is made possible because children's brains have the built-in ability to do it. If we think about it, this makes perfect sense. How could we learn anything if we did not have the innate ability to do so already programmed into the hard drives of our brains? Chomsky calls this innate programming, the **Language Acquisition Device or LAD**. Each human being comes into the world with this operating system already installed in the brain, and its presence is not reliant upon any instruction in language (see *fig. 1.2*). Language will be acquired naturally as the child is exposed to language. Further, all children deduce their own grammatical and syntactic rules for the development of language because all languages have the same basic structures, such as words that indicate people or things, words that indicate action, words that indicate direction, and so on. Chomsky is at odds with the behaviorists in that he disputes that the development of language is based merely on imitation. As a proof that this is not the case, he offers the observation that children are capable of generating an *infinite number original sentences*. If children learned language through imitation only, they would not be able to create new sentence structures (Arnove 442–447).

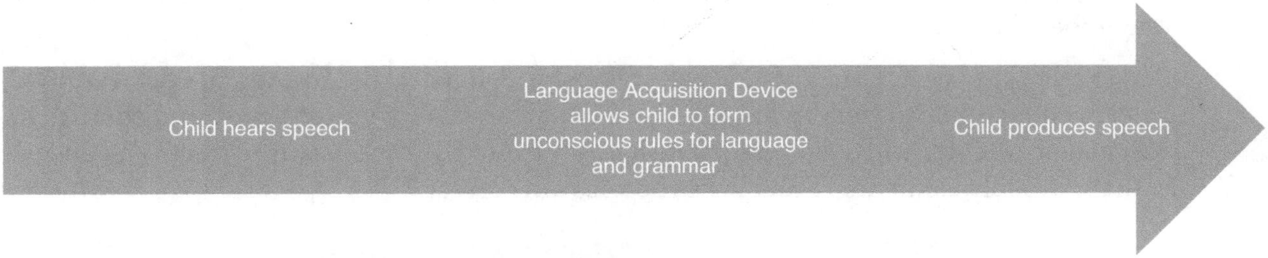

Child hears speech — Language Acquisition Device allows child to form unconscious rules for language and grammar — Child produces speech

Figure 2.   Chomsky's theory of language acquisition.

3. **Social Interactionist Theory (Social Cognitivist Theory)**

   The Social Interactionist Theory is compatible with the **Social Development Theory** of **Lev Vygotsky** (1896–1934) and the **Discovery Learning** Theory of **Jerome Bruner** (1915–2016). The social interactionist theory holds that "language acquisition is influenced by the interaction of a number of factors—physical, linguistic, cognitive, and social" (Cooter and Reutzel 40).

   Constructivism as a teaching and learning philosophy is largely based on Vygotsky's theory, and his development model has come to be known as the sociocultural model. In this model, the social and cultural environment of the child drives the development of language.

This theory somewhat contrasts with those of Chomsky and Piaget in that Vygotsky held that social development precedes cognitive development. In other words, in the acquisition of language, a child first observes language (usually adult language) and then language develops in the child. Learning is dependent upon interaction. Further, Vygotsky described the parameters within which learning takes place as the **zone of proximal development**. The zone of proximal development consists of the range of competency beginning with what the child does not know or understand, progressing to what the child can do with guidance and instruction, and ending with what the child can do independently (see *fig. 1.3*). All learning, including language, takes place within this zone.

Figure 3.   Vygotsky's Zone of Proximal Development.

4. Cognitivist or Cognitive Development Theory

Arguably, no theorist has had more influence on the field of education than **Jean Piaget** (1896–1980.) Piaget proposed that children develop cognitively in **stages** and that much of their learning is dependent upon their physiological and psychological development. Put simply, children are capable of increasingly complex learning as they grow and mature. In terms of language development, this would mean that children learn the complex structures of language on a sort of sliding scale that is commensurate with their level of maturity (see *fig. 1.4*). Conversely, there are levels of learning that cannot occur until the child has moved into the developmental stage that allows it (Matthews 4). While this simplification of Piaget's theory might appear to be no more than an application of common sense, remember that this is only a brief synopsis.

Piaget's work, as well as that of Skinner, Chomsky, Vygotsky, and Bruner, has been studied, scrutinized, and criticized by linguists and behavioral scholars for years, and there is an abundance of literature devoted to just that. Which of the theorists is correct? The answer is that probably elements of all of the theories are correct.

Stage 1	Stage 2	Stage 3	Stage 4
Sensory Motor: Birth to 2 years	Preoperational: 2 to 7 years	Concrete Operational: 7 to 11 years	Formal Operational: 11 years to adult
Explores, observes, and learns through the senses.	Begins to understand symbols. Egocentric. Learning centered on meeting own needs	Begins to understand conservation of matter and classification	Understands abstractions, logic, and systematic thinking.

Figure 4.   Piaget's Stages of Development.

Spoken Language Development

First of all, recognize that there are basically two types of language: **receptive and expressive**. Receptive language is that which we understand, either as it is spoken or as we see it in print, and expressive language is that which we use in speaking and writing. Two other terms often used for these two concepts and that have the same meaning are **active and passive** language. That seems easy enough.

Whatever the mechanisms that allow children to learn language, it is generally agreed that language development occurs in fluid stages. There is some dispute as to how many stages exist, what to call the stages, and particularly the general age range at which the stages occur. Multiple sources exist that divide language acquisition into many stages, sometimes ten or more. Six of the frequently used descriptors of language development are shown below. It is important to note that children, being individuals, develop language at their own individual rates, and thus the ages listed for each stage of development are by no means exact.

Stages in a Child's Development of First (Native) Spoken Language

Preverbal

Prelinguistic or preproduction cooing and babbling, later contains **proto words** or sounds that begin to sound like words *about 3 to 11 months*.

Grammatical

Emergent: First words and **holophrases** (one word), *10 or 11 months to about 1½ years* of Developing; **Protophrases** (two-word sentences): Children learn about the use of language and tone, *1½ years to 2 or older*.

Telegraphic: Short and simple phrases and sentences—like a telegraph, *about 2½ through about 3 years*.

Posttelegraphic or Complex: Grammatically complete sentences, *36 months and older*.

Adult-like structures: Sophisticated sentence production. *About 10 years and continuing through adulthood* (Bochner and Jones 14–24).

Stages in a Child's Development of a Second Spoken Language

The following information is taken from *The Stages of Second Language Acquisition*, a publication of the ASCD:

Preproduction: The child may have receptive language but is not yet speaking. Has minimal comprehension of what is said.

Early Production: Comprehension is limited. The child begins to develop an expressive (active) vocabulary. Uses short responses and phrases. Typically uses present tense verbs.

Speech Emergence: Good comprehension. The child can communicate with simple words and sentences. May not fully understand social language. Makes grammatical errors.

Intermediate Fluency: Excellent comprehension. Few grammatical errors. At this stage, there has been significant growth. The child becomes more vocal and more inclined to share thoughts, ideas, and questions.

Advanced Fluency: This stage approximates the proficiency of the native speaker and may take up to seven years to reach.

Stages in English-Language Learners' Development of Speaking, Reading, and Writing

Given the changing demographic makeup of the United States, it is important that teachers understand how English-language learners (ELLs) develop proficiency in the English language. To this end, the World Class Instructional Design Consortium has developed a taxonomy (set of performance definitions) that describes the stages of language acquisition for ELLs. This framework is used by departments of education in most states. The language acquisition taxonomy and standards can be found at the **WIDA** website at https://www.wida.us/index.aspx. The WIDA has a strict copyright policy related to the reproduction of any of their materials; therefore, the taxonomy and standards are not reproduced in this text. Generally, the performance standards focus on the language competencies necessary in order for children to become successful in school. The standards follow a graduated performance ladder similar to that found in other language arts taxonomies. Like Bloom's, WIDA levels are scaffolded from lowest to highest and are described as **entering, beginning, developing, expanding, bridging, and reaching**. Teacher candidates are required to be familiar with the taxonomy and standards developed by the WIDA both for licensing examinations and in the classroom; therefore, it is highly recommended that candidates visit the WIDA website and become familiar with the appropriate information.

Stages in a Child's Writing Development

There is a correlation between speaking, reading, and writing (Kroll 32–54). Early writing **develops concurrently with early reading.** It is part of the overall understanding of language in children (Schickedanz). There are various labels for the various stages of writing develop. Existing models include five general stages of writing development as the **prephonemic**, the **early phonemic**, the **letter-name, the transitional, and the conventional** (Temple, Nathan, Temple, and Burris; Graves). Each of these stages contains substages that help teachers to identify the child's progression on the literacy spectrum. Children use language skills and acquired understanding of words to help them learn to read, and they use their knowledge of reading to help them learn to write.

The first stage of writing is the emergent stage. Its milestones are described in table 1.1. Recall that the development of all literacy skills in all children is fluid, and children do not abruptly leave one stage and enter another. Nevertheless, it is important for teachers to know the general continuum so as to better instruct children at their developmental levels.

Emergent Writing

Table 1.   Characteristics of the Early (Emergent) Development of Written Language

Drawing	Scribbling	Letter Like Forms	Reproducing Learned Units	Invented Spelling/ Transitional	Conventional Spelling
Picture writing that is purposeful, not random	Purposeful assortment of marks used as if for letters	Begins to actually write letters	Can copy some words but may not understand them	Has learned that letters have sounds and attempts to recreate them	This is a transitional stage in which invented spelling is replaced by correct spelling

Source: Teresa Byington and Kim Yaebin, "Promoting Pre-Schoolers' Emergent Writing" *Young Children*, Vol. 72, 5, November 2017

Stages of a Child's Development in Reading

Obviously, the first stage of literacy development is that of spoken language. A child's spoken language develops prior to his or her use of language in writing or reading. This begins at infancy and continues throughout childhood. Therefore, books read to children should be slightly above their conversational level so that their vocabularies are in a constant state of growth. Harris and Hodges refer to emergent reading as the period of acquisition of skills that make reading possible.

Uta Frith developed a model for the stages of the acquisition of reading. Frith actually studied dyslexia extensively, and much of her research led her to the identification of the typical trajectory of reading development, which benefits all children. Her model enjoys worldwide acceptance and is described in table 1.2.

Table 2.   Uta Frith's Model of the Stages of Reading Development

Frith's Model	
Logographic Stage	At the earliest stage, the child recognizes words by their visual features such as shape and length. Children at this stage can recognize signs like McDonald's. They are not aware that letters represent sounds. Letters are no different to children at this stage than are any other symbols.
Alphabetic Stage	Children at this stage begin to recognize letters as different from other symbols. Letter–sound correlation begins to develop. This is the beginning of the development of phonological skills, and children begin to recognize phonemes. They begin to decode words.
Orthographic Stage	Children have developed a cache of sight words and no longer need to sound out all words. They may sound out unfamiliar words. They have developed a store of graphemes as well and can instantly call them to mind when encountering new words.

Source: Frith, U. "Beneath the surface of developmental dyslexia." *Surface Dyslexia, Neuropsychological and Cognitive Studies of Phonological Reading*, edited by K. Patterson, J. Marshall, and M. Coltheart, Erlbaum, 1985, pp. 301-330.

To recap, we know that spoken language develops prior to reading and writing skills and that reading and writing skills develop simultaneously. We know that growth in reading promotes growth in writing and vice versa. We know that it is important for teachers to understand cognitive developmental theory and to recognize developmental stages in children's acquisition of language so that appropriate instruction can be delivered.

Grammar No. 1

Framework

Why is this information included in a text on teaching children's literature? Writing is an integral component of literacy and flows naturally from the reading of literature. Questions regarding basic grammar appear on most versions of the PRAXIS examination.

Definitions teacher candidates need to know

Grammar: The entire system of language. It includes all the conventions, principles, and rules of the language.

Syntax: The arrangement of words to make sentences.

Inflection: The way we make words sound when we speak. It depends on how the mouth and tongue are shaped as we speak.

Semantics: The meaning that we infer or imply with our choice of words. Sometimes, we can be misunderstood because of the way we use semantics.

Morphology: The study of how words are formed.

Linguistics: The scientific study of language (includes the study of morphology, semantics, and syntax, as well as others).

The Eight Parts of Speech

1. Noun: The name of a person, place, thing, or idea.

2. Pronoun: A word that takes the place of or stands for a noun.

3. Verb: A word that shows action or state of being.

4. Adverb: A word that modifies a verb, adjective, or another adverb.

5. Adjective: A word that describes a noun or a pronoun.

6. Preposition: A word that shows relationship between one word and another.

7. Conjunction: A word used to join words, phrases, and clauses.

8. Interjection: A word used to show excitement or emotion.

Prepositions

A preposition is a word that shows relationship, usually relative to time, place, or direction. Prepositions are usually used to begin prepositional phrases. A prepositional phrase is a group of words containing a preposition, its object, and any modifiers of that object. The object of the preposition is a noun, pronoun, or word acting as a noun or pronoun.

Prepositional phrase indicating time

Alice arrived at noon.

Prepositional phrase: *at noon*

Preposition: *at*

Object of preposition: *noon*.

Prepositional phrase indicating place

Lauren left her cell phone in the car.

Prepositional phrase: *in the car*

Preposition: *in*

Object of preposition: *car*

Prepositional phrase indicating direction

Hickory, Dickory, Dock. The mouse ran *up the clock*.

Preposition: *up*

Object of preposition: *clock*

It is important that students recognize prepositions when they see them. It is also important that they understand that often we determine whether or not a word is a preposition based on how it is used in a sentence. Below is a list of commonly used prepositions:

about	behind	except	off	toward
above	below	excepting	on	under
across	beneath	for	onto	underneath
after	beside(s)	from	out	until
against	between	in	outside	up
along	beyond	inside	over	upon
among	but	in spite of	past	up to

(Continued)

(Continued)

around	by	instead of	regarding	with
as	concerning	into	since	within
at	despite	like	through	without
because of	down	near	throughout	with regard to
before	during	of	to	with respect to

How are prepositional phrases used in sentences?

Generally, prepositional phrases are used to modify verbs, nouns, pronouns, adjectives, or adverbs. If a prepositional phrase modifies a verb, adjective, or adverb, it is an **adverbial** phrase. If a prepositional phrase modifies a noun or a pronoun (or gerund), it is an **adjective** phrase.

Prepositional phrase modifying a verb, adjective, or another adverb: Words that modify verbs, adjectives, and other adverbs are adverbs. Since adverbs generally tell **how**, **when**, **where**, **to what extent**, or **why** about the words they modify, we know that **adverbial phrases**—prepositional phrases used as adverbs—do the same thing. They generally follow the adjectives or adverbs that they modify, but can occur practically anywhere in a sentence when they modify a verb.

Examples:

At some point during the summer, we always go to the beach.

Verb: *go*. Go when? at some point (prepositional phrase modifying verb)

Verb: *go*. Go when? during the summer (prepositional phrase modifying verb)

Verb: *go*. Go where? to the beach (prepositional phrase modifying verb)

My students typically submit their best work early *in the semester*.

Adverb: *early* (modifying the verb: *submit*)

How early? in the semester (prepositional phrase modifying adverb)

Elizabeth is very good *at writing* but is exhausted *by the deadline*.

Adjective in the sentence: good (predicate adjective modifying Elizabeth)

Under what condition is she good? at writing (prepositional phrase modifying adjective)

Prepositional phrase modifying a noun or pronoun: Words that modify nouns or pronouns are adjectives. Since adjectives generally tell **which one**, **what kind**, **how much**, **how many, or under what condition** about the nouns or pronouns they modify, we know that **adjective phrases**—prepositional phrases used as adjectives—do the same thing. They follow the words they modify.

Examples: The man *in the flannel suit* is a spy.

Noun: man. Which man? in the flannel suit (prepositional phrase modifying noun)

He *with the most cash* is king.

Pronoun: he. Which he? with the most cash (prepositional phrase modifying pronoun)

Parting note: The subject of a sentence will NEVER be contained within a prepositional phrase.

Grammar and Writing Websites for Teachers and Students

It is important to know and use these.

The Purdue Owl Writing Lab at https://owl.english.purdue.edu/. This website is not for young students. It is for the teacher, for high school and for college students, but, it will answer virtually any question one may have about grammar, writing, and formatting. It is free.

Brain Pop Grammar at https://www.brainpop.com/english/grammar/. There is no reason not to include grammar exercises and games in the curriculum with the wealth of resources available at this site. Brain Pop is loaded with activities for students. It even includes diagraming sentences—that archaic practice that we have been told for years was, well, archaic. It can be argued that diagraming is one of the best ways to truly understand the structure of a sentence. Requires subscription.

Grammar Bytes at http://www.chompchomp.com/menu.htm. This is an amazingly rich website that includes presentations, handouts, exercises, and interactive exercises for children. It is free.

Grammarly Handbook at https://www.grammarly.com/blog/category/handbook/. This is a very helpful site with information about the basics of grammar and writing as well as an opportunity for students to have their text reviewed. It is free.

Quill at https://www.quill.org/. This site is very helpful in the teaching of writing. It is loaded with resources that will help children with their writing. Free to teachers and students.

Chapter 2

A Brief History of Children's Literature

Alignments

▶ International Literacy Association: Standard 2.1
▶ InTASC, Standards: 4. l, 4.o, 5.r
▶ ETS, Praxis Exam: 5002 b *Test Specifications*
▶ WIDA (World Class Instructional Design and Assessment :) Standard 2
▶ NCTE/CAEP: 1.1, 2.2

Framework

All written literature began with the oral tradition; stories told orally and passed down from generation to generation. Early humans used marks and picture symbols to tell stories and to keep track of things (like time passing, number of animals killed) but, based on archeological research, it is believed that written language first appeared in Mesopotamia in about 3100 BCE (Fagan and Beck 762). Written language then followed in other civilizations. There is an entire science devoted to the study of the development of writing, and many researchers debate where the first writing actually occurred, but the central idea for our purpose in this text is to acknowledge the logical concept that language preceded writing, and writing preceded literature.

The Development of Literary Texts

The oldest known literary texts are probably the "Kesh Temple Hymn," and the "Instructions of Shuruppak," both written around 2500 BCE in Sumeria. The oldest known piece of written fiction is the "**Epic of Gilgamesh**," which also appeared in Sumeria in the third millennium BCE (Hallo 63). Ancient texts were obviously not intended for widespread use. There was usually one copy only, and that copy was carefully guarded and preserved. During the Middle Ages, monks in Catholic monasteries made a great contribution to the world by copying ancient texts. Often these monks or scribes made copies of the Bible, but they also copied other Greek and Latin texts. Sometimes, monks copied books for wealthy patrons who paid the church for the service. During this time as in previous times, written texts of any type were usually the property of governments, churches, or wealthy individuals, and texts were few and far between (Books before Gutenberg). For centuries, people have used folktales and fables to both instruct and entertain children. Initially, the stories were told orally, and many of them continue to thrive in the oral tradition today. Aristotle (384–322 BCE) referenced a man named **Aesop** who reputedly was born in 620 BCE in Thrace. It is the traditional belief that Aesop was a slave who somehow managed to gain his freedom. Aesop gained a reputation for being the originator of a great many fables. Written versions of the fables (in Greek) date back to the sixteenth–tenth centuries BCE. It is unknown whether Aesop actually authored all the fables for which he is given credit. Among the at least 725 of Aesop's fables are *The Ant and the Grasshopper*, *The Boy Who Cried Wolf*, *The Goose That Laid the Golden Eggs*, *The Town Mouse and the Country Mouse*, and *The Tortoise and the Hare* (Simondi).

Printed Manuscripts

In 1439, Johannes Gensfleisch zur Laden zum **Gutenberg** invented movable type and adapted it to some existing technology (possibly a wine press) to form the printing press. Gutenberg made the widespread distribution of books, pamphlets, and newspapers possible and is credited with ushering in the Age of Mass Communication. Many scholars argue that the availability of printed material to the masses was a contributing factor to the Renaissance in Europe, while others argue that the spread of print was more a result of the Renaissance than a cause (Einstein 42–88). In either case, Gutenberg's role in the dawning of this new age cannot be overstated. For example, Gutenberg's historical importance is acknowledged on the Arts and Entertainment Network's listing of the *100 Most Influential People of the Millennium*, where his name appears first on the list. Gutenberg is followed by Isaac Newton, Martin Luther, Charles Darwin, and William Shakespeare at numbers 2–5. Gutenberg is also first in A and E's *Biography's* list of the most important people of the millennium.

Not surprisingly, the first mass produced and mass distributed book in Europe was the Gutenberg Bible in 1455. Other books followed both in Europe and other parts of the world. William Caxton (1422–1491) became the first publisher in England. He published what is believed to be the first book of stories printed in England. Caxton's *The Recuyell of the Historyes of Troye*, published in 1464, is a translation from the French of stories about the Trojan Wars by Raoul Lefèvre, a French writer. Caxton also published Sir Thomas Mallory's *Le Morte d'Arthur* (The Death of King Arthur), and an English version of *Aesop's Fables* in 1484. Around 1485, an illustrated Italian version of Aesop's fables was printed in Brescia, Italy. The printer used woodcuts for illustrations. The book described Aesop's life and also contained many of his fables (Learning Timeline). A copy of this book is housed in the Library of Congress in the Rare Book and Special Collections Division.

Books for Children

It is not difficult to imagine that with the dearth of printed material prior to and during the Middle Ages (ca. fifth–fifteenth centuries), most people could not read, and the books that were available to be read to children or read by them were written for adults. There were some exceptions. For example, printed in France in 1487, *Les Contenances de la Table*, a book on table manners by Jean Du Pre, was probably the first printed book intended specifically to be read by or to children. By 1640, the literacy rate in England has been estimated to have risen to about 30% among males (Spufford 27).

As the literacy rate rose, a market for cheap books for the working class developed, and a new type of publication, later called **chapbooks**, became popular. Chapbooks were cheaply made books made of folded paper, usually with no cover. The books usually consisted of eight–twenty-four pages, and the writing frequently contained errors. They were sold by peddlers (chapmen) on the streets, in markets, at fairs, and sometimes door-to-door. In England, these books usually cost a half-penny or even less. Because they were so cheaply made, few survive today (Spufford 107–130). Although most chapbooks were not written for children, there were some that contained stories that we typically associate with children, such as *The History of Jack the Giant Killer*, and *Tom Thumb, His Life and Death*. Free online versions of both of these chapbooks are available at the following website: https://archive.org/details/McGillLibrary-PN970_K49_T6_1840-1220. The popularity of chapbooks continued in both Europe and America through the mid-1800s.

Probably the first widely distributed English printed books for children were religious books or catechisms, intended to instruct children in the beliefs of the church. In 1646, *Milk for Babes: Drawn out of the Breasts of Both Testaments* was published in England. The American version by John Cotton, a minister of the Church of England, was published in Boston in 1656. The title of Cotton's book was *Spiritual Milk for Boston Babes in Either England: Drawn out of the Breasts of Both Testaments*. This book contained the teachings of Puritanism and later became a part of the *New England Primer*. It remained in use for 200 years (Royster).

Orbis Sensualium Pictus, or The World of Things Obvious to the Senses Drawn in Pictures is considered by many to be the first printed picture book for children. Published in Germany in both Latin and German in 1648, it was translated into English in 1659 by Johann Amos **Comenius**. *The Orbis*, the shortened version of the title, was an educational book for children (Orbis Sensualium Pictus). The first lessons pertain to the alphabet, and the remainder of the book consists of lessons for living. It concludes with a final chapter entitled, "The Last Judgment." Some chapters of *The Orbis* are socially insensitive by modern standards. Topics that would surprise today's readers include the Biblical account of Adam and Eve, the outward parts of man and woman, dice games, beer making, the torture of prisoners or "malfactors," and a description of people with disabilities, called "deformed and monstrous people." That said, most of the book is made up of basic lessons that were designed to instruct children in good behavior and to provide them with at least a passing knowledge of basic science, philosophy, geography, and theology, including descriptions of the three primary religions of Europe at the time. The book also includes descriptions of the major trades practiced by the working classes of Europe (McNamara). A free online version of this book is available at the following web address: https://archive.org/details/johamoscommeniio00comee.

The **Hornbook** was used in England as early as the fifteenth century and in the New England Colonies as early as the 1600s. Interestingly, it wasn't a book at all. It was typically a piece of wood, leather, or other material with a printed page containing the alphabet, possibly with a list of vowel and consonant blends, and often with the Lord's Prayer, all on one page. The page was laminated

© Time Life Pictures/Contributor/Getty

Figure 2. The Hornbook.

with a thin sheet of cow, oxen, or sheep horn so that it could be handed down from child to child. The horn was soaked in water so that it became pliable and thin sheets of usable keratin were peeled away from the bone. The keratin sheets were then heated in boiling water and pressed with heavy plates or other flat objects to make them transparent. The hornbook typically had a handle and looked like a paddle (Plimpton) (see fig. 2.1).

Between 1687 and 1690, Benjamin Harris, a British journalist and American immigrant published *The New England Primer*. A book of less than hundred pages, the Primer was written specifically to educate school-aged children. In fact, as early as 1642, Massachusetts Law required that all children be taught literacy (Royster). The Primer was somewhat like Comenius' *The Orbis* in that it contained woodcuts and moral lessons. The text was meant to teach children literacy through religious reading, and thereby instruct them in the tenets of Calvinism. A free online version this book is available at the following website: https://archive.org/details/newenglandprimer00fordiala.

It is worth noting that childhood as a separate stage of life from adulthood is a relatively modern concept. In early modern England (ca. 1500–1800), many children did not live to adulthood. Diseases such as dysentery, scarlet fever, whooping cough, smallpox, measles, and influenza were rampant, not to mention the occasional outbreak of plague. Childhood deaths from accidents were also common. Children were expected to work at home if they lived in rural areas or in apprenticeships or paid employment if they were city dwellers. Children were considered employable at around the age of 8. Many children died of accidents connected with farm work or work from dangerous employment such as blacksmithing or serving on ships (Payne). It is generally estimated that one in four children did not live to reach the age of 15, and the greatest number of childhood deaths occurred from disease during the first year of life (Sommerville).

If one survived childhood, adult life expectancy was also short. In Elizabethan England, life expectancy was between 30 and 40 years. It follows that children were considered to be adults at a much younger age than in modern times. Consider that Shakespeare's Juliet, from *Romeo and Juliet*, was 13 years old. In English Common Law, the age of sexual consent in 1576 was set to 10 years. In America in the 1700s, the age of consent varied between 10 and 12 years, depending upon the state (ABA 67).

NEW ENGLAND PRIMER TABLE OF CONTENTS

John Locke, an English philosopher, is included in this history because of his treatise, written in 1693, *Some Thoughts Concerning Education*. Written for an aristocratic friend who was bringing up a son, Locke penned the most influential educational philosophy of his time. He advocated three basic tenets: a sound body, a sound mind, and an appropriate education. Locke posited that parents should watch their children and follow their interests and aptitudes in the planning of their education: "He, therefore, that is about children, should well study their natures and aptitudes and see, by often trials, what turn they easily take and what becomes them, observe what their native stock is, how it may be improved, and what it is fit for" (Locke, *Some Thoughts*, 41). Locke further posited that children should learn through play and that learning should be fun. "They must not be hinder'd from being children, or from playing, or doing as children, but from doing ill; all other liberty is to be allow'd them" (Locke, *Some Thoughts*, 69). "Children should not have any thing like work, or serious, laid on them; neither their minds, nor bodies will bear it" (Locke, *Some Thoughts*, 149).

Several new ideas stood out in Locke's work related to the education of children. For one thing, he offered the idea that children should be allowed to be children and not treated as little adults. The concept of childhood as a separate and important part of life was a relatively new social construct, as was the idea that play was important for learning and development. It is worth noting that even the casual observer of nature is aware that all mammals learn through play and that childhood play has a purpose. Consider the African lion, often the subject of nature films and research studies. The lion cub learns the tactics of hunting by playing with its siblings, hunting, stalking, and pouncing. Likewise, we should not need a theorist to point out to us that children learn through imaginative and imitative play. We have all been children, and we know that we learn from interaction with adults and through play with other children. Further, play occurs naturally, without prompting from adults. Physical skills and agility grow in this way as do the acquisition of language and social skills.

Notwithstanding Locke's admonitions related to the teaching of children, children's books tended to remain largely instructional until the mid-1700s. F. J. Harvey Darton, an authority on children's books has written that prior to 1770 children's books were intended to instruct children or to teach them to behave. There were few if any books written to interest or entertain children(Montanaro). However, there were a few books written to entertain children prior to 1770. These include *Tales of Mother Goose*, *The Tommy Thumb Songbook*, *Beauty and the Beast, and The History of Little Goody Two*

Shoes (see Milestones in the History of Children's Literature timeline). Another important event in the world of children's literature occurred in 1765. During that year, Robert Sayer, an English publisher began to publish mechanical books for children. These books were initially known as harlequin books because of the harlequin figure that appeared in the early versions. Mechanical books frequently contained pages that were divided into paper sections containing pictures. These sections might be lifted or slid to the side to produce a picture. **Pop-up books** were and are a version of this art form. These books were made solely for the purpose of entertaining children and gaining their attention. They were, and remain, very popular (Montanaro).

In a similar vein to Locke's work, Jean-Jacques **Rousseau** (1712–1778), a Swiss-born philosopher who worked mostly in France, also felt that learning should be fun for children and should follow their interests. Rousseau believed that young boys should be educated in the natural world as much as possible and that education from books should be secondary. He believed in learning from experiences and interaction with a tutor (Arbuthnot 34). With regard to the education of girls, Rousseau took a different tack. Women were to be educated so as to be lead, not to be leaders. Rousseau was an extremely controversial figure. Topics about which he wrote included music, the natural state of man, art, education, and religion. He published numerous books on numerous topics, including what many consider to be the progenitor of the modern autobiography. Several of his books that were critical of religion were banned. Politically, he leaned toward socialism and opposed such things as private property. He was a contradiction in terms regarding the education of children as well. He, himself, had five children with his mistress, a seamstress by the name of Thérèse Levasseur. Rousseau and his mistress did not raise any of their children, but rather left all of them at the Paris orphanage soon after birth. Nevertheless, Rousseau was and is revered as one of the great philosophers, and his work, *Emile*, a semi-fictitious novel in which he revealed his views on education had a major impact on the development of children's literature (Jean-Jacques Rousseau article).

Toward the end of the eighteenth century, the market for children's books became firmly established. Books remained primarily instructional or didactic until the mid-nineteenth century when Lewis Carroll's (also known as Charles Lutwidge Dodson, Oxford mathematician) landmark fantasy for children, *Alice's Adventures in Wonderland*, was published. This book intrigued the imagination of children, and as such, signaled the beginning of the First Golden Age of Children's Literature (Knowles and Malmkjaer). In England, early illustrators of children's books began to gain great recognition toward the end of the nineteenth century. Among these were **Randolph Caldecott, Walter Crane, and Kate Greenaway**. In 1902, Beatrix Potter, an English writer, both wrote and illustrated *The Tale of Peter Rabbit*. Potter is generally credited with being the first author of children's books to use illustrations that were of equal importance to the content of the story. She published twenty-three children's books in all and is revered as both a writer and illustrator to this day. Other notable books by English authors from the Golden Age were Kenneth Grahame's, *The Wind in the Willows*, published in 1908 and the founder of Boy Scouts, Robert Baden Powell's *Scouting for Boys*, published in the same year. Frances Hodgson Burnett credited *Scouting for Boys* as part of her inspiration for her classic, *The Secret Garden*, published in 1910.

It is often said that the Golden Age of children's literature ended in Europe with World War I and did not gain steam again until after World War II. However, a number of significant works were published during these years. Among them were *Winnie the Pooh*, by A. A. Milne in 1926; *Mary Poppins*, by P. L. Travers in 1934; and J. R. R. Tolkein's, *The Hobbit* in 1937. Puffin Books also made their debut during World War II. These were the first paperback books for children, and they made reading for pleasure affordable for the middle and lower classes. After World War II, children's books again flourished.

In the United States, publication of children's books went into overdrive after the end of the Civil War in 1865. In 1868, Louisa May Alcott's *Little Women* introduced a new genre, the coming of age story. **May Hill Arbuthnot** in *Children and Books*, 1964, referred to *Little Women* as an "epoch-making" book (Arbuthnot 113–114). In 1900, the American writer, L. Frank Baum published his classic, *The Wonderful Wizard of Oz*. In 1922, the American Library Association began awarding the Newbery Medal. The Caldecott Medal followed in 1932. Dr. Seuss published his first book in 1937, *And to Think I Saw it all on Mulberry Street*. In 1952, E. B. White's *Charlotte's Web* was published, and it was an instant success. Maurice Sendak began writing and illustrating books in the 1960s, the most famous of which is the award winning, *Where the Wild Things Are. Harriet the Spy* by Louise Fitzhugh followed in 1964.

Although children's books of note became so numerous from the mid-twentieth century forward that they are too numerous to describe in this context, one series of note must be mentioned. From 1997 through 2007, British author J. K. Rowling produced the greatest selling series of books of all time. The *Harry Potter* series is read worldwide and has been translated into 67 languages. Its popularity shows no signs of slowing down.

Milestones in the History of Children's Literature

8th century BCE Classical Greek and Roman Myths

620–560 BCE Life of Aesop

1439 Gutenberg invents movable type and the printing press

1476 William Caxton establishes printing business

1570 *A Method or Comfortable Beginning for All Unlearned* by John Hart (first known alphabet book with pictures)

ca. 1640 Chapbooks became popular in England

1659 *Orbis Sensualium Pictus* by Johann Amos Comenius

1660 *A Little Book for Little Children* by Thomas White, didactic of Protestant ideals

1678 *The Pilgrim's Progress* by John Bunyan

ca. 1687–1690 *New-England Primer*, Publication in Boston

1693 *Some Thoughts Concerning Education* by John Locke

1719 *Robinson Crusoe* by Daniel Defoe

1726 *Gulliver's Travelers* by Jonathan Swift

1729 *Tales of Mother Goose* (English version) by Charles Perrault

1744 *A Little Pretty Pocket Book* by John Newbery

1744 *Tommy Thumb's Song Book* by Mary Cooper (nursery rhymes)

1761 *Beauty and the Beast* (English translation) originally by Mme Leprince Debeaumont (1757)

1762 *Emile: or On Education* by Jean Jacques Rousseau

1765 *The History of Little Goody Two-Shoes* by John Newbery (original version credited to Oliver Goldsmith—thought to be the first book written to amuse children.)

1765 The first mechanical or pop-up books for children were published in England by Robert Sayer. They were referred to as metamorphosis books or harlequin books because of the harlequin figure that appeared in the early versions (Montanaro).

1785 First American edition of *Mother Goose's Melodies*

1812 *Fairytales* by Jacob and Wilhelm Grimm

1812 *The Swiss Family Robinson* by Johann David Wyss

1819 *Rip Van Winkle* and *The Legend of Sleepy Hollow* by Washington Irving

1823 *A Visit from St. Nicholas* by Clement C. Moore

1834 *McGuffey Readers* began to be published in America

1837 *Andersen's Fairy Tales* by Hans Christian Andersen

1843 *A Christmas Carol* by Charles Dickens

1846 *Wonderful Stories for Children* by Hans Christian Andersen, translated by Mary Howitt

1863 *Cinq semaines en ballon, voyage de découvertes en Afrique* (*Five Weeks in a Balloon*) by Jules Verne (science fiction)

1865 *Alice's Adventures* in Wonderland by Lewis Carroll

1868 *Little Women* by Louisa May Alcott

1868 *Heidi* by Johanna Spyri (Switzerland) with part II in 1869

1878 Randolph Caldecott's first "Toy Books"

1879 *Under the Window* by Kate Greenaway

1880 *Uncle Remus, His Songs and Sayings*, the folklore of the old plantation by Joel Chandler Harris (fables of African-Americans-considered racist and stereotypical today, but very popular in its day. Disney made a movie called *Song of the South* using these tales).

1881 *Treasure Island* by Robert Louis Stevenson

1883 *The Adventures of Pinocchio* by Carlo Collodi

1883 *The Merry Adventures of Robin Hood* by Howard Pyle

1884 *The Adventures of Huckleberry Finn* by Mark Twain (some find it objectionable today because of the racial terms used in the book. The theme is much more complicated and viewed by many as anti-racist as Twain deliberately emphasized the absurdity of the racist practices of the time).

1885 *A Child's Garden of Verses* by Robert Louis Stevenson

1894–1895 *The Jungle Book* by Rudyard Kipling

1899 *Little Black Sambo* by Helen Bannerman

1900 *The Wizard of Oz* by L. Frank Baum

1902 *The Tale of Peter Rabbit* by Beatrix Potter

1903 *The Story of King Arthur and His Knights* by Howard Pyle

1903 *The Call of the Wild* by Jack London

1904 *Peter Pan* by J. M. Berrie, Scottish

1934 *Dick and Jane* basal reading series first publication, concept developed by Zerna Sharp, an elementary teacher, and William S. Gray. May Hill Arbuthnot was also a contributor. This reading series was used for 35 years before it fell out of favor during the 1960s. The books are still very popular and are again available, selling millions of copies, mostly to parents (Gabriel).

1940 Puffin Books first paperback books for children released in England

1958 *A Bear called Paddington* by Michael Bond

1961 *James and the Giant Peach* by Roald Dahl

1962 *The Snowy Day* by Ezra Jack Keats (groundbreaking because the story is about a young African American child in an urban setting).

1963 *A Wrinkle in Time* by Madeleine L'Engle

1963 *Where the Wild Things* Are by Maurice Sendak

1967 *The Outsiders* by S. E. Hinton young adult, coming of age book that became enormously popular)

1968 *The Very Hungry Caterpillar* by Eric Carle

1970 *Are You There, God? It's Me, Margaret* by Judy Blume

1971 *The Planet of Junior Brown* by Virginia Hamilton—focus is on African American child

1974 *The Chocolate War* by Robert Cormier

1976 *Ashanti to Zulu* by Leo and Diane Dillon

1976 *Roll of Thunder, Hear My Cry* by Mildred D. Taylor

1977 *Bridge to Terabithia* by Katherine Paterson

1997 *Harry Potter and the Philosopher's Stone* (US title: *Harry Potter and the Sorcerer's Stone*) by J. K. Rowling (best-selling young people's books of all time)

Grammar Review No. 2

Nouns

Noun: Names a person, place, thing, or idea

A common noun names a general person, place, thing, or idea and is not capitalized.

Examples: teacher, forest, cat, freedom

Common nouns are sometimes broken down into categories. These are *concrete, abstract, and collective.*

Concrete nouns name things that exist physically and can be perceived by the senses.

Examples: land, bike, mountain

Abstract nouns name things that cannot be detected with the senses.

Examples: integrity, love, hope (these are ideas)

Collective nouns name a collection of persons, places, things, or ideas, *but collective nouns are singular nonetheless and take singular verbs.*

Example: The *group is going* to the game.

A proper noun names a particular person, place, or thing (ideas are not typically proper nouns).

Examples: Mrs. Carter, Cherokee National Forest, Buffy

Usage of Nouns in Sentences

Usage of nouns in a sentence: subject, direct object, indirect object, objective of the infinitive, object of a preposition, subject complement (predicate nominative), object complement, appositive, or adjective

Noun used as subject:

The *girl* on the bus would not take a seat.

Noun used as direct object:

The batter struck the *ball* with resounding force.

Noun used as indirect object:

Mom gave my *sister* the keys to the car.

Noun used as objective of an infinitive:

The patient is not allowed to eat solid *foods* for six days.

Noun used as object of a preposition:

The mouse ran under the *chair*.

Noun used as a subject complement (predicate nominative):

Alice is an amazing *singer*.

Noun used as an object complement: An object complement *can* be *either* a noun or an adjective that follows the direct object and renames it. In this case, we are looking at nouns used as object complements. Unlike an appositive, an object complement is not set off by a comma.

The committee named Mr. Jones *President*.

Noun used as an appositive: An appositive is a noun or noun phrase that renames another noun right beside it in the sentence.

My sister, a *doctor*, told me to refrain from foods high in saturated fat.

Noun used as an adjective: Sometimes nouns are used as adjectives. A noun used as an adjective always comes right before the noun it modifies.

Mrs. Duncan is the best *history* teacher in the school.

Noun of direct address: This is always a proper noun and is set off by a comma. It is the name of a person being spoken to in a sentence and has no other grammatical function in the sentence.

Ralph, will you please clean your room?

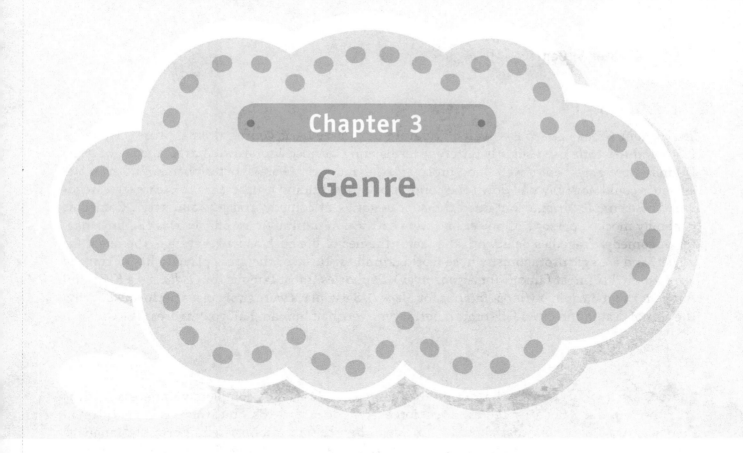

Chapter 3

Genre

Alignments

▶ International Literacy Association: Standard 2.1
▶ InTASC, Standards: 4.a, 4.l, 4.r
▶ ETS, Praxis Exam: 5002 b *Test Specifications*,
▶ NCTE/CAEP: Standard 1

Framework

This chapter is devoted to the topic of genre in literature. The focus is on the conventional genres (the plural of "genre" can be either "genres" or "genre") which all language arts teachers must know and understand. Children's literature itself is broken into genre and formats, and they are explored in Chapter 7.

The word "genre" simply means category. It applies to all types of art, including, but not limited to, music, painting, and writing. Categorizing literary genre is not a simple task. Genre is a broad and ever-broadening term, the clear definition of which does not seem to be generally agreed upon by scholars, artists, publishers, or the public at large. In fact, it is difficult to find a consensus as to even the broad major categories. Then, there is the issue of subgenre and exactly what constitutes a subgenre. Even if the various genres could be clearly defined, the process of placing works of literature strictly into one category or another can prove troublesome. Finally, there is the dilemma of distinguishing type from form.

Our working definition of genre will assume that literature of a certain genre will share basic traits and that the same will apply to subgenres.

The Origin of the Concept of Genre

The ancient Greeks generally divided literature into three basic genres: drama, prose, or poetry. Plato and Aristotle used slightly different terms and classified literature as drama, epic, or lyric. Dramas were plays, epics were long prose stories, and lyrics were shorter poems. But even the ancients could not fully nail down the concept of genre, finding it necessary to create subcategories. For example, drama contained the subcategories of comedy, tragedy, and satyr. Comedies generally mocked persons of power and were satirical in nature. Aristophanes was the first master of comedy. Tragedies dealt with the major themes of life such as love, revenge, the quest for power, and a tragic protagonist whose world crumbles. Three of the great playwrights of tragedy were Aeschylus (most famous for *Agamemnon*), Sophocles (most famous for *Oedipus the King*, and *Antigone*), and Euripides ((most famous for *Medea*). Satyr plays were short plays performed during the acts of drama and provided comic relief. Satyrs were half human–half goat figures (The Greeks).

Genre Today

There is a school of thought that posits that genre classification is completely unnecessary. It is true that a universally accepted classification system does not exist, but there is general agreement as to the elements that should be included in a classification system. Certainly, language arts teachers must have a working knowledge of the types and subtypes of literature. This chapter provides classifications and definitions that will assist teachers.

For our purposes in this text, we will identify the major genres as **prose, poetry, drama**, and **media**. Each of the four main genres contains genre divisions or subgenres (table 3.1).

Table 1.   Prose

I. PROSE—Language as it is spoken		
Genres		
Fiction		**Nonfiction**
Form 1. *Literary*— Distinguishable from commercial by style and sometimes by the quality of writing.	Form 2. *Commercial (or Genre fiction)*. Appeals to a broad audience and may require less mental investment than literary. Read for entertainment. It should be noted that some commercial literature can also be considered literary and of high quality.	Writing that focuses on real people or events.

I. PROSE—Language as it is spoken		
Genres		
Types of Literary Fiction	**Types of Commercial Fiction**	**Types of Nonfiction**
Romance, in the classic sense means a story involving extraordinary exploits and heroes. It may or may not contain a love story. Example: *Le Morte d'Arthur* by Sir Thomas Mallory	Romance, in the modern sense may or may not contain extraordinary exploits and heroes, but usually contains a love story. Example: *The Thorn Birds* by Colleen McCullough	Biography Autobiography Essay ◆ **Persuasive**—to make an argument in order to convince ◆ **Expository**—to convey information ◆ **Narrative**—to tell a story, must have characters and plot ◆ **Descriptive**—to paint a picture ◆ **Creative**—original, expressive writing 　Journal 　Speech 　Diary 　Memoirs 　Technical writing 　Interviews 　News writing 　Opinion pieces 　Letters 　Literary criticism 　Textbooks
Western Literary Example: *Lonesome Dove* by Larry McMurtry	Western Commercial Example: *Where the Wild Horses Roam* by Duane Boehm	Western Nonfiction Example: *Bury my Heart at Wounded Knee* by Dee Brown
Mystery Literary Example: *The Complete Sherlock Holmes* by Sir Arthur Conan Doyle	Mystery, Modern Commercial Example: *The Firm* by John Grishom	Mystery Nonfiction Example: *And the Sea Will Tell*, by Vincent Bugliosi

(Continued)

I. PROSE—Language as it is spoken

Genres

Science Fiction Literary Example: *The Time Machine* by H. G. Wells	Science Fiction Commercial Example: *Divergent* by Veronica Roth	Science Nonfiction Example: Scientific Paper
Horror Literary Example: *Dracula* by Bram Stoker	Horror Commercial Example: *The Shining* by Stephen King	Horror Nonfiction Example: *In Cold Blood*, by Truman Capote
Mythology Literary stories and legends about real or imagined people. Examples: *Greek, Roman, and Norse Mythology*, focuses on ancient gods and goddesses.	Mythology Commercial Example: *Tarzan*	
Fantasy Literary Example: *The Lion, the Witch, and the Wardrobe* by C. S. Lewis	Fantasy Commercial Example: *The Harry Potter Series* by J. K. Rowling	
Graphic Novel Literary: Example: *Jane Eyre* by Charlotte Bronte	Modern Gothic Novel Commercial etc. Example: *Interview with the Vampire*, by Anne Rice	

This text distinguishes between types and forms of poetry, but the terms "type" and "form" are not universally agreed upon and are sometimes interchanged. NOTE: *Many poems can be classified as more than one type.* Examples are provided for study so that candidates may review the elements of poetry. When example text was too long for inclusion, portions of poems were used, and candidates should access the entire versions online for further study. All poems are public domain (table 3.2).

Table 2. Poetry

II. Poetry literature that uses style and rhythm to express intense feelings. It may or may not rhyme.	
Types	**Definitions and Examples**
Narrative	A Poem that Tells a Story. It must have a **plot and characters**. Example: Edgar Allen Poe's *The Raven*, Public domain. Once upon a midnight dreary, while I pondered, weak and weary, Over many a quaint and curious volume of forgotten lore— While I nodded, nearly napping, suddenly there came a tapping, As of some one gently rapping, rapping at my chamber door. "'Tis some visitor," I muttered, "tapping at my chamber door— Only this and nothing more." Ah, distinctly I remember it was in the bleak December; And each separate dying ember wrought its ghost upon the floor. Eagerly I wished the morrow;—vainly I had sought to borrow From my books surcease of sorrow—sorrow for the lost Lenore— For the rare and radiant maiden whom the angels name Lenore— Nameless *here* for evermore.
Narrative	And the silken, sad, uncertain rustling of each purple curtain Thrilled me—filled me with fantastic terrors never felt before; So that now, to still the beating of my heart, I stood repeating "'Tis some visitor entreating entrance at my chamber door— Some late visitor entreating entrance at my chamber door;— This it is and nothing more." Presently my soul grew stronger; hesitating then no longer, "Sir," said I, "or Madam, truly your forgiveness I implore; But the fact is I was napping, and so gently you came rapping, And so faintly you came tapping, tapping at my chamber door, That I scarce was sure I heard you"—here I opened wide the door;— Darkness there and nothing more. Deep into that darkness peering, long I stood there wondering, fearing, Doubting, dreaming dreams no mortal ever dared to dream before; But the silence was unbroken, and the stillness gave no token, And the only word there spoken was the whispered word, "Lenore?" This I whispered, and an echo murmured back the word, "Lenore!"— Merely this and nothing more. Back into the chamber turning, all my soul within me burning, Soon again I heard a tapping somewhat louder than before.

(Continued)

Table 2. Poetry (*Continued*)

II. Poetry literature that uses style and rhythm to express intense feelings. It may or may not rhyme.	
Types	**Definitions and Examples**
	"Surely," said I, "surely that is something at my window lattice; Let me see, then, what threat is, and this mystery explore— Let my heart be still a moment and this mystery explore;— 'Tis the wind and nothing more!"
Narrative	Open here I flung the shutter, when, with many a flirt and flutter, In there stepped a stately Raven of the saintly days of yore; Not the least obeisance made he; not a minute stopped or stayed he; But, with mien of lord or lady, perched above my chamber door— Perched upon a bust of Pallas just above my chamber door— Perched, and sat, and nothing more. Then this ebony bird beguiling my sad fancy into smiling, By the grave and stern decorum of the countenance it wore, "Though thy crest be shorn and shaven, thou," I said, "art sure no craven, Ghastly grim and ancient Raven wandering from the Nightly shore— Tell me what thy lordly name is on the Night's Plutonian shore!" Quoth the Raven "Nevermore." Much I marvelled this ungainly fowl to hear discourse so plainly, Though its answer little meaning—little relevancy bore; For we cannot help agreeing that no living human being Ever yet was blessed with seeing bird above his chamber door— Bird or beast upon the sculptured bust above his chamber door, With such name as "Nevermore." But the Raven, sitting lonely on the placid bust, spoke only That one word, as if his soul in that one word he did outpour. Nothing farther then he uttered—not a feather then he fluttered— Till I scarcely more than muttered "Other friends have flown before— On the morrow *he* will leave me, as my Hopes have flown before." Then the bird said "Nevermore."
Narrative	Startled at the stillness broken by reply so aptly spoken, "Doubtless," said I, "what it utters is its only stock and store Caught from some unhappy master whom unmerciful Disaster Followed fast and followed faster till his songs one burden bore— Till the dirges of his Hope that melancholy burden bore Of 'Never—nevermore'."

II. Poetry literature that uses style and rhythm to express intense feelings. It may or may not rhyme.

Types	Definitions and Examples
	But the Raven still beguiling all my fancy into smiling, Straight I wheeled a cushioned seat in front of bird, and bust and door; Then, upon the velvet sinking, I betook myself to linking Fancy unto fancy, thinking what this ominous bird of yore— What this grim, ungainly, ghastly, gaunt, and ominous bird of yore Meant in croaking "Nevermore." This I sat engaged in guessing, but no syllable expressing To the fowl whose fiery eyes now burned into my bosom's core; This and more I sat divining, with my head at ease reclining On the cushion's velvet lining that the lamp-light gloated o'er, But whose velvet-violet lining with the lamp-light gloating o'er, *She* shall press, ah, nevermore! Then, methought, the air grew denser, perfumed from an unseen censer Swung by Seraphim whose foot-falls tinkled on the tufted floor? "Wretch," I cried, "thy God hath lent thee—by these angels he hath sent thee Respite—respite and nepenthe from thy memories of Lenore; Quaff, oh quaff this kind nepenthe and forget this lost Lenore!" Quoth the Raven "Nevermore."
Narrative	Prophet!" said I, "thing of evil!—prophet still, if bird or devil!— Whether Tempter sent, or whether tempest tossed thee here ashore, Desolate yet all undaunted, on this desert land enchanted— On this home by Horror haunted—tell me truly, I implore— Is there—*is* there balm in Gilead?—tell me—tell me, I implore!" Quoth the Raven "Nevermore." "Prophet!" said I, "thing of evil!—prophet still, if bird or devil! By that Heaven that bends above us—by that God we both adore— Tell this soul with sorrow laden if, within the distant Aidenn, It shall clasp a sainted maiden whom the angels name Lenore— Clasp a rare and radiant maiden whom the angels name Lenore." Quoth the Raven "Nevermore." "Be that word our sign of parting, bird or fiend!" I shrieked, upstarting— "Get thee back into the tempest and the Night's Plutonian shore! Leave no black plume as a token of that lie thy soul hath spoken! Leave my loneliness unbroken!—quit the bust above my door! Take thy beak from out my heart, and take thy form from off my door!" Quoth the Raven "Nevermore."

(Continued)

Table 2.   Poetry (*Continued*)

II. Poetry literature that uses style and rhythm to express intense feelings. It may or may not rhyme.	
Types	**Definitions and Examples**
	And the Raven, never flitting, still is sitting, *still* is sitting On the pallid bust of Pallas just above my chamber door; And his eyes have all the seeming of a demon's that is dreaming, And the lamp-light o'er him streaming throws his shadow on the floor; And my soul from out that shadow that lies floating on the floor Shall be lifted—nevermore!

Lyric	A poem that expresses the author's personal feelings about a
	    subject.
	Example: *O Captain, My Captain*, by Walt Whitman. Public domain
	
	O Captain! my Captain! our fearful trip is done;
	The ship has weather'd every rack, the prize we sought is won;
	The port is near, the bells I hear, the people all exulting,
	While follow eyes the steady keel, the vessel grim and daring:
	But O heart! heart! heart!
	O the bleeding drops of red,
	Where on the deck my Captain lies,
	Fallen cold and dead.
	
	O Captain! my Captain! rise up and hear the bells;
	Rise up - for you the flag is flung - for you the bugle trills;
	For you bouquets and ribbon'd wreaths - for you the shores
	    a-crowding;
	For you they call, the swaying mass, their eager faces turning;
	Here Captain! dear father!
	This arm beneath your head;
	It is some dream that on the deck,
	You've fallen cold and dead.
	
	My Captain does not answer, his lips are pale and still;
	My father does not feel my arm, he has no pulse nor will;
	The ship is anchor'd safe and sound, its voyage closed and done;
	From fearful trip, the victor ship, comes in with object won;

Lyric	Exult, O shores, and ring, O bells! But I, with mournful tread, Walk the deck my Captain lies, Fallen cold and dead.

II. Poetry literature that uses style and rhythm to express intense feelings. It may or may not rhyme.

Types	Definitions and Examples
Epic	A long poem about a hero or heroes and their adventures. Example: *Beowulf*, An Anglo-Saxon Epic Poem, Translated From The *Heyne-Socicn* Text by Lesslie Hall. (first sixteen lines) Public domain Lo! the Spear-Danes' glory through splendid achievements The folk-kings' former fame we have heard of, How princes displayed then their prowess-in-battle. Oft Scyld the Scefing from scathers in numbers From many a people their mead-benches tore. Since first he found him friendless and wretched, The earl had had terror: comfort he got for it, Waxed 'neath the welkin, world-honor gained, Till all his neighbors o'er sea were compelled to Bow to his bidding and bring him their tribute: An excellent atheling! After was borne him A son and heir, young in his dwelling, Whom God-Father sent to solace the people. He had marked the misery malice had caused them That reaved of their rulers they wretched had Erstwhile Long been afflicted.
Elegy	A serious poem commemorating the dead Example: Thomas Gray's, *Elegy Written in a Country Churchyard*. (First four stanzas) Public domain The curfew tolls the knell of parting day, The lowing herd wind slowly o'er the lea, The plowman homeward plods his weary way, And leaves the world to darkness and to me. Now fades the glimm'ring landscape on the sight, And all the air a solemn stillness holds Save where the beetle wheels his droning flight, And drowsy tinklings lull the distant folds; Save that from yonder ivy-mantled tow'r The moping owl does to the moon complain Of such, as wand'ring near her secret bow'r, Molest her ancient solitary reign.

(Continued)

Table 2. Poetry (*Continued*)

II. Poetry literature that uses style and rhythm to express intense feelings. It may or may not rhyme.	
Types	**Definitions and Examples**
	Beneath those rugged elms, that yew-tree's shade, Where heaves the turf in many a mould'ring heap, Each in his narrow cell forever laid, The rude forefathers of the hamlet sleep.
Ballad	A simple story, often meant to be sung Example: *The Ballad of Barbara Allen*, Old Irish ballad, Author unknown It was in and about the Martinmas time, When the green leaves were a falling, That Sir John Graeme in the west country Fell in love with Barbara Allan. O Hooly, hooly rose she up, To the place where he was lying, And when she drew the curtain by, 'Young man, I think you're dying.' O it's I'm sick, and very, very sick, And 't is a' Barbara Allan:' 'O the better for me ye's never be, Tho your heart's blood were a spilling. O dinna ye mind, young man,' said she, 'When ye was in the tavern a drinking, That ye made the healths gae round and round, And slighted Barbara Allan?' He turned his face unto the wall, And death was with him dealing: 'Adieu, adieu, my dear friends all, And be kind to Barbara Allan.' And slowly, slowly raise she up, And slowly, slowly left him, And sighing said, she coud not stay, Since death of life had reft him.
Ballad	She had not gane a mile but two When she heartd the death-bell ringing, And every jow that the death-bell geid, It cry'd, Woe to Barbara Allan! 'O mother, mother make my bed! O make it saft and narrow! Since my love died for me to-day, I'll die for him to-morrow.'

II. Poetry literature that uses style and rhythm to express intense feelings. It may or may not rhyme.

Types	Definitions and Examples
Ode	A lyric poem, often written in lofty terms of praise for someone or something. Usually, but not always serious. Example: John Keats' *Ode on a Grecian Urn* Public domain The last two lines are frequently quoted. Thou still unravish'd bride of quietness, Thou foster-child of silence and slow time, Sylvan historian, who canst thus express A flowery tale more sweetly than our rhyme: What leaf-fring'd legend haunts about thy shape Of deities or mortals, or of both, In Tempe or the dales of Arcady? What men or gods are these? What maidens loth? What mad pursuit? What struggle to escape? What pipes and timbrels? What wild ecstasy? Heard melodies are sweet, but those unheard
Ode	Are sweeter; therefore, ye soft pipes, play on; Not to the sensual ear, but, more endear'd, Pipe to the spirit ditties of no tone: Fair youth, beneath the trees, thou canst not leave Thy song, nor ever can those trees be bare; Bold Lover, never, never canst thou kiss, Though winning near the goal yet, do not grieve; She cannot fade, though thou hast not thy bliss, For ever wilt thou love, and she be fair! Ah, happy, happy boughs! that cannot shed Your leaves, nor ever bid the spring adieu; And, happy melodist, unwearied, For ever piping songs for ever new; More happy love! more happy, happy love! For ever warm and still to be enjoy'd, For ever panting, and for ever young; All breathing human passion far above, That leaves a heart high-sorrowful and cloy'd, A burning forehead, and a parching tongue. Who are these coming to the sacrifice? To what green altar, O mysterious priest, Lead'st thou that heifer lowing at the skies, And all her silken flanks with garlands drest? What little town by river or sea shore,

Table 2.   Poetry (*Continued*)

II. Poetry literature that uses style and rhythm to express intense feelings. It may or may not rhyme.	
Types	**Definitions and Examples**
Ode	Or mountain-built with peaceful citadel, Is emptied of this folk, this pious morn? And, little town, thy streets for evermore Will silent be; and not a soul to tell Why thou art desolate, can e'er return. O Attic shape! Fair attitude! with brede Of marble men and maidens overwrought, With forest branches and the trodden weed; Thou, silent form, dost tease us out of thought As doth eternity: Cold Pastoral! When old age shall this generation waste, Thou shalt remain, in midst of other woe Than ours, a friend to man, to whom thou say'st, "Beauty is truth, truth beauty," – that is all Ye know on earth, and all ye need to know.
Dramatic Monologue	A poem in which one person speaks, presumably to an audience. Example: *Ulysses*, by Alfred Lord Tennyson, Public domain It little profits that an idle king, By this still hearth, among these barren crags, Match'd with an aged wife, I mete and dole Unequal laws unto a savage race, That hoard, and sleep, and feed, and know not me.
Dramatic Monologue	I cannot rest from travel: I will drink Life to the lees: All times I have enjoy'd Greatly, have suffer'd greatly, both with those That loved me, and alone, on shore, and when Thro' scudding drifts the rainy Hyades Vext the dim sea: I am become a name; For always roaming with a hungry heart Much have I seen and known; cities of men And manners, climates, councils, governments, Myself not least, but honour'd of them all; And drunk delight of battle with my peers, Far on the ringing plains of windy Troy I am a part of all that I have met; Yet all experience is an arch wherethro' Gleams that untravell'd world whose margin fades For ever and forever when I move.

II. Poetry literature that uses style and rhythm to express intense feelings. It may or may not rhyme.

Types	Definitions and Examples
	How dull it is to pause, to make an end, To rust unburnish'd, not to shine in use! As tho' to breathe were life! Life piled on life Were all too little, and of one to me Little remains: but every hour is saved From that eternal silence, something more, A bringer of new things; and vile it were For some three suns to store and hoard myself, And this gray spirit yearning in desire
Dramatic Monologue	And this gray spirit yearning in desire To follow knowledge like a sinking star, Beyond the utmost bound of human thought. This is my son, mine own Telemachus, To whom I leave the sceptre and the isle – Well-loved of me, discerning to fulfil This labour, by slow prudence to make mild A rugged people, and through soft degrees Subdue them to the useful and the good. Most blameless is he, centred in the sphere Of common duties, decent not to fail In offices of tenderness, and pay Meet adoration to my household gods, When I am gone. He works his work, I mine. There lies the port: the vessel puffs her sail: There gloom the dark broad seas. My mariners, Souls that have toiled, and wrought, and thought with That ever with a frolic welcome took The thunder and the sunshine, and opposed Free hearts, free foreheads – you and I are old; Old age hath yet his honour and his toil; Death closes all; but something ere the end, Some work of noble note, may yet be done, Not unbecoming men that strove with Gods. The lights begin to twinkle from the rocks: The long day wanes: the slow moon climbs: the deep Moans round with many voices.

(Continued)

Table 2. Poetry (*Continued*)

II. Poetry literature that uses style and rhythm to express intense feelings. It may or may not rhyme.	
Types	**Definitions and Examples**
Dramatic Monologue	Come, my friends, 'Tis not too late to seek a newer world. Push off, and sitting well in order smite the sounding furrows; for my purpose holds To sail beyond the sunset, and the baths Of all the western stars, until I die. It may be that the gulfs will wash us down: It may be that we shall touch the Happy Isles, And see the great Achilles, whom we knew. Though much is taken, much abides; and though We are not now that strength which in old days Moved earth and heaven; that which we are, we are; One equal temper of heroic hearts, Made weak by time and fate, but strong in will To strive, to seek, to find, and not to yield.
Idyll	A short pastoral poem describing the virtues of a place, time, person, or other subject. Example: *The Solitary Reaper*, by William Wordsworth, Public domain Behold her, single in the field, Yon solitary Highland Lass! Reaping and singing by herself; Stop here, or gently pass! Alone she cuts and binds the grain, And sings a melancholy strain; O listen! for the Vale profound Is overflowing with the sound.
Idyll	No Nightingale did ever chaunt More welcome notes to weary bands Of travellers in some shady haunt, Among Arabian sands: A voice so thrilling ne'er was heard In spring-time from the Cuckoo-bird, Breaking the silence of the seas Among the farthest Hebrides. Will no one tell me what she sings?— Perhaps the plaintive numbers flow For old, unhappy, far-off things, And battles long ago:

II. Poetry literature that uses style and rhythm to express intense feelings. It may or may not rhyme.

Types	Definitions and Examples
	Or is it some more humble lay, Familiar matter of to-day? Some natural sorrow, loss, or pain, That has been, and may be again? Whate'er the theme, the Maiden sang As if her song could have no ending; I saw her singing at her work, And o'er the sickle bending;— I listened, motionless and still; And, as I mounted up the hill, The music in my heart I bore, Long after it was heard no more.
Aubade	A morning love poem or a poem about lovers who must separate at dawn. Example: Shakespeare's Hark, Hark, the lark from Cymbeline, Act II, Scene iii Public domain Hark, hark! the lark at heaven's gate sings, And Phoebus 'gins arise, His steeds to water at those springs On chaliced flowers that lies; And winking Mary-buds begin To ope their golden eyes: With every thing that pretty is, My lady sweet, arise: Arise, arise. *Cymbeline*, Act II, Scene III
Pastoral	A poem originally idealizing the life of the shepherd, but later including the idealization of country life. Many pastoral poems are quite long. Example: *Lines Composed a few miles above Tintern Abbey*, (first two stanzas) by William Wordsworth. Public domain Five years have passed; five summers, with the length Of five long winters! and again I hear These waters, rolling from their mountain-springs With a soft inland murmur. Once again

(Continued)

Table 2.   Poetry (*Continued*)

II. Poetry literature that uses style and rhythm to express intense feelings. It may or may not rhyme.	
Types	**Definitions and Examples**
Pastoral	Do I behold these steep and lofty cliffs, That on a wild secluded scene impress Thoughts of more deep seclusion; and connect The landscape with the quiet of the sky The day is come when I again repose Here, under this dark sycamore, and view These plots of cottage-ground, these orchard-tufts, Which at this season, with their unripe fruits, Are clad in one green hue, and lose themselves 'Mid groves and copses.Once again I see These hedgerows, hardly hedgerows, little lines Of sportive wood run wild; these pastoral farms, Green to the very door; and wreaths of smoke Sent up, in silence, from among the trees! With some uncertain notice, as might seem Of vagrant dwellers in the houseless woods, Or of some Hermit's cave, where by his fire The Hermit sits alone.
Epigram	A short, clever poem, usually consisting of two to four lines. (Not all epigrams are poems. Epigrams can also be short, terse statements.) Example by Samuel Taylor Coleridge Public domain. Sir, I admit your general rule, That every poet is a fool, But you yourself may serve to show it, That every fool is not a poet.
Epitaph	A tombstone inscription, usually pointed. Example: (The author saw this on a tombstone once.) As you are, I once was. As I am, you soon will be.
Confessional	A style of poetry that arose during the 1950s. It deals with the extreme personal emotions of the poet. These are poems in which the poet bares his or her soul and provides personal information that would not otherwise be known to the public. Because the confessional movement began fairly recently, no copy is provided here. For an example of this style of poetry, research the works of Sylvia Plath, Robert Lowell, or Anne Sexton.

II. Poetry literature that uses style and rhythm to express intense feelings. It may or may not rhyme.	
Types	**Definitions and Examples**
Didactic	Poems that are meant to teach a lesson or to lecture. Many poets have included didactic poetry in their repertories, and even nonpoets have contributed to the canon of didactic poetry. Didactic poems can consist of a couple of lines or multiple stanzas and can be lyrics, sonnets, or virtually any other type of poem. Example: by Benjamin Franklin Little strokes Fell Great Oaks

Forms of Poetry

Poetry type in this text is distinguished as pertaining to the nature of the poem; in other words, what the poem is meant to do or convey. Form in poetry is defined here as poetry that conforms to a specific structure, or in the case of free verse, has no structure and can be of any type.

Sonnet, English or Shakespearean: A fixed poem of fourteen lines, usually in iambic pentameter, consisting of three quatrains and a couplet.

Example: Shakespeare's *Sonnet 116* (complete poem)

Let me not to the marriage of true minds
Admit impediments. Love is not love
Which alters when it alteration finds,
Or bends with the remover to remove:
O, no! it is an ever-fixed mark,
That looks on tempests and is never shaken;
It is the star to every wandering bark,
Whose worth's unknown, although his height be taken.
Love 's not Time's fool, though rosy lips and cheeks
Within his bending sickle's compass come;
Love alters not with his brief hours and weeks
But bears it out even to the edge of doom.
If this be error, and upon me prov'd,
I never writ, nor no man ever lov'd

Italian or Petrarchan Sonnet: A fixed poem of fourteen lines, usually in iambic pentameter, consisting of an octave and a sestet. ababcdcd-efefgg rhyme scheme

Example: *Sonnet* by Dante Alighieri, translated by D. G. Rosetti (complete poem)

Ye ladies, walking past me piteous-eyed,
Who is the lady that lies prostrate here?
Can this be even she my heart holds dear?
Nay, if it be so, speak, and nothing hide.
Her very aspect seems itself beside,
And all her features of such altered cheer

That to my thinking they do not appear
Hers who makes others seem beatified.

If thou forget to know our lady thus,
Whom grief o'ercomes, we wonder in no wise,
For also the same thing befalleth us,
Yet if thou watch the movement of her eyes,
Of her thou shalt be straightaway conscious.
O weep no more; thou art all wan with sighs.
(Trans. D.G. Rossetti)

Villanelle: A fixed poem of nineteen lines, consisting of five tercets and a quatrain. One of the best examples of this type of poem is that of Dylan Thomas' *Do not Go Gentle into that Good Night*; however, this poem is not in the public domain. It is often quoted, and can be easily located on the Internet.

Example: *The House on the Hill* by Edward Arlington Robinson

They are all gone away,
The House is shut and still,
There is nothing more to say.

Through broken walls and gray
The winds blow bleak and shrill:
They are all gone away.

Nor is there one to-day
To speak them good or ill:
There is nothing more to say.

Why is it then we stray
Around that sunken sill?
They are all gone away,

And our poor fancy-play
For them is wasted skill:
There is nothing more to say.

There is ruin and decay
In the House on the Hill:
They are all gone away,
There is nothing more to say.

Free Verse Poetry with no rhyme scheme or pattern. This form of poetry is tricky to identify because it *may rhyme*, but it will not have a *rhyme scheme*.

Blank Verse *Unrhymed* lines of iambic pentameter

Haiku A poem developed by the Japanese, consisting of three unrhymed rhymes of five, seven, and five syllables. An example is provided in the chapter on children's poetry.

Limerick A humorous poem of five lines with the rhyme scheme aabba. Some are obscene. An example is provided in the chapter on children's poetry.

Websites: Teachers can find public domain poems at several websites. One recommended website http://www.public-domain-poetry.com/ has more than 38,000 poems arranged in a **user-friendly format**. Poems in this section were accessed at this website.

Table 3. Drama

III. Drama, literature that is meant to acted (Note: Not all drama can be classified; for example, Thornton Wilder's *Our Town*).	
Type	**Definition**
Comedy	Plays that are meant to be humorous and have happy endings. Example: Shakespeare's *A Midsummer Night's Dream*
Tragedy	Plays of a darker tone that do not have happy endings. The protagonist has a tragic character flaw that leads to his or her demise. Example: Shakespeare's *Macbeth*
History	Some scholars do not recognize history as a type of drama. It is included here because Shakespeare wrote histories as well as comedies and tragedies. Shakespeare's histories were generally tragedies, but also contained comedy. Example: Shakespeare's *Richard III*
Farce	Plays that use exaggerated humor; nonsense Example: Oscar Wilde's *The Importance of Being Ernest*
Melodrama	Plays (or films) that are designed to appeal to the viewer's emotions. Example: George Bernard Shaw's adaptation of *Pygmlion*
Musical	Plays that use music to tell the story. Example: Andrew Lloyd Webber's *Phantom of the Opera* Some reviewers consider all operas to be musicals, but not all musicals are operas.

Table 4. Media

IV. Media—Generally, media encompasses the genres of fiction and nonfiction, with the primary difference being the method of delivery; namely, film or some version of film.			
Types			
Drama	Comedy	Science Fiction	Horror
Fantasy	Documentary	Romance	Thriller
Action/Adventure	Crime	Animation	

Grammar Review No. 3

Verbs

It's complicated. A verb is a word that implies action or state of being (linking). Definitions can be confusing *because* often the determinate of whether a verb is an action or linking verb is how the verb is used in a sentence. The following are examples of verbs that can be either action or linking: look, feel, smell, taste, remain, grow, and act.

Types of Verbs

Action Verbs: These verbs imply some type of action rather than state of being. The action can be physical or mental. Examples: run, think, wish, write, pray, and ride

Action Verbs are either *Transitive or Intransitive*

Transitive Verb: has a direct object

Example: Tom *ate* the entire pie. (Subject: Tom) (action [and transitive] verb: ate) (direct object: pie)

Intransitive Verb: does not have a direct object

Example: The dog *ran* out the door. (Subject: bug) (action [and intransitive] verb: ran) (no direct object)

Linking Verbs: These verbs are also called state of being verbs for lack of any better descriptors. They are called linking verbs because they link the subject of a sentence to a subject complement. Subject complements take the form of predicate nominatives (nouns) or predicate adjectives, or pronouns.

Examples: look, feel, sound, taste, seem, prove, remain, and grow

Linking Verb linked to an adjective:

Examples:

Her mom *was* happy that she could visit for Mother's Day. (subject: mom) (linking verb: was) (predicate adjective: happy)

Her mother *seemed* exhausted when she arrived. (Subject: mother) (linking verb: seemed) (predicate adjective: exhausted)

Linking Verb linked to a (predicate nominative/noun)

That kid *is* a hot mess. (Subject: kid) (linking verb: is) predicate noun: mess)

Linking Verb linked to a pronoun:

The fault appears to be mine. (Subject: fault) (linking verb: appears) (predicate pronoun: mine)

The Linking Verbs that are called Verbs of Being are usually forms of the verb: to be

Examples:

> is
> am
> are
> were
> was
> are being
> has been
> had been
> will be

So, how can some verbs are used as either action or linking verbs? Here are some *examples*:

The roast *smells* delicious (linking). Smell is **linking** the subject, cookies, to the adjective, heavenly.

I smelled it as soon as it was taken out of the oven (action)

Helping Verbs: (also called auxiliary verbs) help the main verb to convey time. In other words, they "help" the main verb to tell when something happened, is happening, or will happen. Sometimes helping verbs help main verbs to show possibility. Often forms of the verb: to be are used as helping verbs. Helping verbs are located immediately before the main verb in a sentence.

Examples:

Elizabeth *can* type faster than anyone I know. (Can is the helping verb to the main verb: type)

I *will be* going to Lowes today. (Will be is the helping verb to the main verb: going)

Verbs have Tense

Simple Present: Amy *runs* in marathons.

Present Perfect: Amy *has run* in many marathons (running started in the past).

Present Progressive: Amy *is looking* for more marathons to run (looking is an ongoing action in the present).

Present Perfect Progressive: Amy has been looking for new marathons since March (looking began in the past and is ongoing).

Simple Past: Amy *ran* in the Boston Marathon (running was done in the past and has been completed).

Past Perfect: Amy *had run* in many marathons before the last one (running occurred in the past prior to another action).

Past Progressive: Amy *had been running* before the local marathon was instituted (running was ongoing in the past but has ended).

Simple Future: Amy *will run* in next week's marathon (running will happen in the future).

Future Perfect: Amy *will have run* in 100 marathons before she retires (running will occur in the future and will be completed at a certain point).

Future Progressive: Amy will be running in marathons in marathons for the next three weeks (running will start in the future and will be ongoing for some amount of time).

Future Perfect Progressive: In April, Amy will have been running in marathons for seven years (running is an ongoing action that will be completed at a certain point).

Verbs have Mood

Indicative Mood: indicates factuality

Example: Mary *sits* at the bus stop each day.

Imperative Mood: indicates command

Example: *Get* out of my way

Interrogative Mood: indicates questioning

Example: *Will* you *please* loan me a pencil?

Conditional Mood: indicates something that will result in something else. It uses words like *might and could*.

Example: My head *might explode* if I hear that speaker again.

Subjunctive Mood: indicates a supposition or a statement contrary to fact.

Example: If I *were* famous, I would hire a body guard. Note that the subjunctive mood uses a plural verb with a singular subject (singular subject: I) (plural verb: were). The subjunctive mood is the only time this occurs. Note further that many people no longer use the subjunctive mood.

Verbs have Number

That means that, like nouns, they can be either singular or plural. This is particularly important in the realm of subject–verb agreement. Singular subjects must take singular verbs, and plural subjects must take plural verbs. Interestingly, in the present tense, most plural nouns end in s, and most plural verbs do not.

- ◆ The student runs to school every day. Singular subject (student), singular verb (runs)
- ◆ The students walk to school every day. Plural subject (students), plural verb (walk)

Verbs have Voice

Verbs are either in the **Active** or the **Passive** Voice.

A verb in the active voice performs the action of the subject

Example: The *coach threw* the ball to the player (subject: coach) (active verb: threw)

A verb in the passive voice actually performs the action on the subject.

The ball was thrown to the player by the coach (subject: ball) (passive voice verb: was thrown)

Verbals

Verbals are special forms of verbs that function as other parts of speech.

Gerund: A gerund is a verbal ending in ing and used in any way that a noun can be used in a sentence (subject, direct object, object of preposition, predicate nominative, appositive, etc.)

Example: *Painting* is my favorite hobby (used as subject)

I enjoy *painting* (used as direct object)

Participle: A participle is a verbal ending in ing and used an adjective.

Present participles end in ing. Past participles usually end in ed or en.

Example: The *rushing* stream is beautiful.

The *written* word is a powerful force.

Infinitive: An infinitive is a verb form with the word "to" coming directly before it or implied as coming directly before it. They are used as adjectives, adverbs, or noun.

Chapter 4

Literary Elements and Literary Devices

Alignments

▶ International Literacy Association: Standard 2.1
▶ InTASC, Standards: 4.a, 4.l, 4.r
▶ ETS, Praxis Exam: 5002 b *Test Specifications*,
▶ NCTE/CAEP: Standard 1

Framework

What is the difference in a literary element and a literary device? As with many aspects of literature, there is no fixed set of literary elements or literary devices, or even a general agreement as to the definition of the two terms. For learning purposes, we will try to make a distinction between the terms. Think of literary elements as we would think of the periodic table of elements in chemistry. Literary elements are the building blocks of literature, particularly fiction. They are universal, and if they are not present, a piece of literature is incomplete, if it is literature at all. Literary devices, on the other hand, are techniques that writers use to make their writing vivid and interesting. The important thing is to know and understand the terms and to recognize them when we see them in literature. Being able to do so will enable us to teach these devices to children for the purpose of enhancing their understanding and enjoyment of literature and, hopefully, to use these tools in their own creative writing. Specific classification of the terms into categories is less important.

Literary Elements

It is generally agreed that the following are the basic elements of fiction.

I.   **Plot** The sequence of events in a story. The different elements of plot follow.

   A.   *Introduction (or Exposition)*: The primary characters and plot are introduced. Sometimes the major conflict is provided in the introduction, and sometimes it unfolds over time.

   B.   *Narrative Hook*: The point in the story, hopefully early on, at which the author grabs the reader's attention and makes the reader want to continue reading.

   C.   **Conflict**: The struggle between opposing characters or forces in the story. Types of conflict follow.

      1.   *Internal*: Conflict within a character (character vs. self)

      2.   *External*: Conflict between a character and an outside force.

         a.   Character versus character

         b.   Character versus nature or other entity

   D.   **Rising Action**: When the central conflict begins to build.

   E.   **Climax**: The turning point or the point at which the conflict reaches its most suspenseful point.

   F.   **Falling Action**: The events that occur after the climax and help to lead toward resolution.

   G.   *Resolution*: The final plot element. The conflict concludes in an outcome, whether happy or unhappy.

II.   **Characters**: The people or animals (or things) which the story is about. There are different types of characters.

   A.   **Protagonist**: The main character in a story.

   B.   **Antagonist**: The character who is at odds with the protagonist or other characters.

      1.   **Dynamic** *Character*: One who changes in the story.

      2.   **Static** *Character*: One who does not change, regardless of events.

      3.   **Flat** *Character*: One who has one or two traits.

      4.   **Round** *Character*: One who has several facets to behavior and personality.

      5.   *Stock Character*: One that is instantly recognizable as a stereotype, such as a nerd, a schoolyard bully, an absent minded professor, and so on.

      6.   *Archetypal Character*: A stock character that appears over and over in literature, such as a mother figure, a mentor, a rebellious child, and so on. There is little, if any, real distinction between stock and archetypal characters.

      7.   *Foil*: A character that illuminates the traits of another character through contrast. For example, the evil witch in *Snow White* helps to show the goodness of *Snow White*.

8. *Confidante*: A character in whom another character confides, thus revealing information about the confiding character.

9. *Indirect characterization*: Occurs when the author allows the reader to discover the character's nature and personality through reading about his or her thoughts, words, and deeds.

10. *Direct characterization*: Occurs when the author just tells the reader directly about the character. For example: "John was a brave and good man."

III. **Theme**: The overall message of the story. It reveals the author's purpose in writing the story.

IV. **Setting**: The place and time in which a story takes place.

V. **Point of View**: Point of view is sometimes defined as an element of fiction. It refers simply to the perspective from which the story is told and has four main subdivisions.

A. *First person, singular*: Uses the pronoun, *I*. **The main character is telling the story**. For example: "I woke up, having no idea what had transpired the night before."

B. *First person, plural*: Uses the pronoun, *we*. Collective individuals are telling the story. For example: "We all went to the funeral that morning, and returned home for tea." This is a very uncommon point of view.

C. *Second person*: **Uses the pronoun, *you*, as if the narrator is speaking directly to you**. For example: "You already know the story of Rapunzel, but let me tell you what really happened."

D. *Third person limited*: Uses the pronouns he, she, and they. **The story is being told, as if it were filmed**. The information provided to the reader is *limited*, in that the reader only gets to fully know the main character through his or her thoughts and actions.

E. *Third person omniscient*: Uses the pronouns he, she, and they. The word *omniscient* means all-knowing and seeing, so the reader is able to see into the thoughts of any character and move about in time in the story if the author chooses.

VI. **Style**: An author's distinct way of writing. It is developed through the author's choice of words, syntax, cadence, theme, and other elements and devices.

Literary Devices or Techniques

This list is by no means all inclusive. There are literally hundreds of literary devices.

1. ***Alliteration***: The repetition of the same first consonant sound in words. Example: *Peter Piper picked a peck of pickles*.

2. *Allusion*: A reference to something else in literature, history, mythology, or the Bible (or others such as sports) that the reader should recognize. Example: *He was a regular Babe Ruth that day*.

3. *Anaphora*: Repeating the same word or words at the beginning of phrases or clauses for effect. Example: *Mad world! Mad kings! Mad composition!* (Shakespeare, *King John*, II, i)

4. **Aphorism**: A short, terse statement conveying wisdom. Example: A bird in the hand is worth two in the bush.

5. **Apostrophe**: (not the punctuation mark) An address to someone or something. Example, John Donne's *O Death, be not proud.*

6. **Assonance**: Repetition of the same vowel sounds in a line or successive lines. "On either side of the river lie, Long fields of barley and of rye." Alfred Lord Tennyson's *The Lady of Shalot.*

7. **Anthromorphism**: Ascribing human traits to a nonhuman creature or object.

8. *Atmosphere*: The general feeling that the writer creates. Example: eerie in *The Legend of Sleepy Hollow* by Washington Irving

9. **Cacophony**: A loud combination of sounds.

10. *Colloquialism*: An expression in common language, often but not always regional. Example: *That dog won't hunt.*

11. **Consonance**: Repetition of the same consonant sound in words that appear in the same line or lines that are close together. Consonance can appear anywhere in a word; while alliteration refers to the repetition of beginning sounds. Example: "Till then sit still, my soul: foul deeds will rise through all the earth o'erwhelm them, to men's eyes." Shakespeare's *Hamlet.*

12. *Dialect*: Speech specific to a geographic region. Example: *fixin'* Appalachian dialect for getting ready to.

13. *Diction*: Speaking style, includes word choice.

14. *Ellipsis*: Omission of one or more words that the reader will assume.

15. *Enjambment*: Continuing one line of poetry into the next line without punctuation

16. *Epiphany*: A sudden realization or manifestation

17. *Epistrophe*: Repetition of one or more words at the end of phrases or clauses. *Example: government of the people, by the people, and for the people.* Lincoln, Gettysburg Address

18. **Euphemism**: A polite or more palatable way of saying something. Example: *passed away* instead of *died.*

19. **Foreshadowing**: A hint in a piece of literature of something that will happen later

20. *Hubris*: Arrogance, often without foundation

21. **Hyperbole**: Gross exaggeration. Example: I will die if I don't get to go to the concert.

22. **Idiom**: An expression for which the meaning is different from the meaning of its words. Example: *beat around the bush.*

23. **Imagery**: The picture that a writer paints with words

24. **Irony**: An outcome that is the opposite of what would be expected or follow naturally. Example: *He used so much hand sanitizer that it made him sick.*

25. *Juxtaposition*: Placing two things beside each other for contrast. A split screen on the evening news showing the opulence of a royal wedding on one side and London tenements on the other.

26. *Kenning*: Describing something in two words linked by a hyphen. Example: pig-skin

27. *Metonymy*: Substituting an attribute of something for the thing itself. Example: Calling our car our ride.

28. **Metaphor**: A comparison without the use of the words like or as. Example: *She's a peach*.

29. **Mood**: The general feeling created in the reader by the writer.

30. **Motif**: Repetition of the same object or word throughout a piece of literature. Example: *illness* in *The Fall of the house of Usher* by Edgar Allen Poe

31. **Onomatopoeia**: Using words that sound like their meaning. Examples: *swish, boom, pop*

32. **Oxymoron**: A contradiction in terms. Example: *open secret*

33. *Paradox*: Using words that seem to contradict themselves, but upon closer inspection, contain some truth. Example: *Life is much too important to be taken seriously*. Oscar Wilde.

34. **Parallelism**: Similarity of structure in a sentence.

35. *Periphrasis*: Using far too many words to convey simple meaning.

36. **Personification**: Giving human qualities to nonhuman entities. Example: *The dish ran away with the spoon*. Mother Goose

37. **Point of View**: The viewpoint from which the story is told. First person, Second Person, or Third Person is the generally accepted definition, BUT, we have noted some sources that equate point of view with the writer's attitude toward the story, which we call *tone* in this text.

38. *Portmanteau*: The process of joining together two or more words to create a new word while retaining the meaning of both. Example: Tabloids called Brad Pitt and Angelina Jolie, "Branjolina."

39. **Pun**: A play on words to convey more than one meaning. Example: *The book about insomnia was a real snoozer*.

40. *Satire*: Making fun of human weaknesses. Example: television's, *The Simpsons* is highly satirical.

41. **Simile**: A comparison of two things using like or as. Example: *Float like a butterfly, sting like a bee*. Mohammed Ali

42. *Stream of consciousness*: The process of writing exactly as the mind thinks, often without complete thoughts, flowing from one topic to the next. Example: James Joyce's, *Ulysses*

43. **Synecdoche**: Substituting a part for the whole. Example: *I want some new wheels*.

44. **Tone**: The writer's attitude toward the audience.

Grammar Review No. 4

Standard Pronouns

Pronouns are words that can take the place of nouns or substitute for them in sentences.

Personal Pronouns

Subjective pronouns are pronouns that can be used as subjects of sentences or clauses:

Singular Subjective	Plural Subjective
First Person: I	we
Second Person: you	you
Third Person: he, she, it	they

Objective pronouns are pronouns that can be used as objects of and prepositions:

Singular Objective	Plural Objective
First Person: me	us
Second Person: you	you
Third Person: him, her, it	they

Possessive pronouns are pronouns that show ownership:

Singular Possessive	Plural Possessive
First Person: my, mine	Our, ours
Second Person: your, yours	Your, yours
his, hers	their, theirs

Reflexive pronouns are pronouns that "reflect" or refer back to the subject of a clause:

Singular Reflexive	Plural Reflexive
First Person: myself	Ourselves
Second Person: yourself	Yourselves
Third Person: himself, herself	themselves

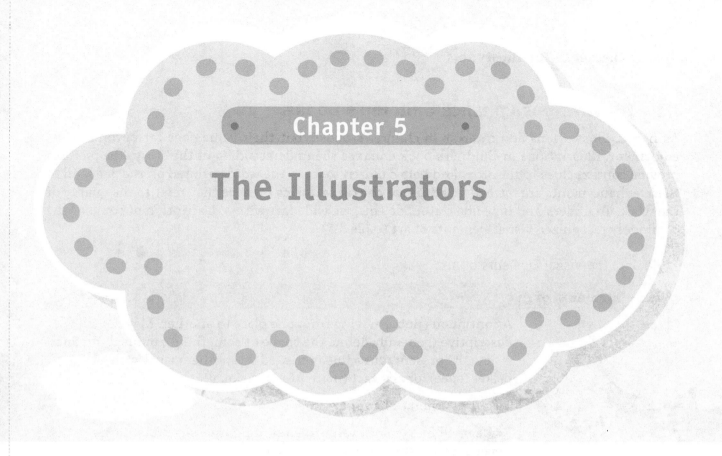

Chapter 5

The Illustrators

Alignments

▶ International Literacy Association: Standard 2.1
▶ InTASC, Standards: 4.a, 4.l, 4.r
▶ ETS, Praxis Exam: 5002 b *Test Specifications*,
▶ NCTE/CAEP: Standard 1

Framework

Illustration in children's books is an art form. We don't need researchers to tell us that children respond to pictures and illustrations. We know that even infants respond to images, and anyone who has ever shown a picture book to a young child has seen the response. Children, like most people, enjoy visual stimuli. Many, if not most of us, if we are honest can admit that as adults, we still like children's books. C. S. Lewis said, "When I was ten, I read fairy tales in secret and would have been ashamed if I had been found doing so. Now that I am fifty, I read them openly." Think of a favorite picture book. Would the book be as enjoyable if it contained only text?

How Illustrations Enhance Children's Books

As noted, illustrations add interest to children's books, but their value goes far beyond visual enjoyment. Illustrations in children's book enhance the understanding of the story. The pictures provide context clues to the story and help children to learn the words printed on the page. All of these enhancements are termed **qualitative characteristics** because they refer to the quality of the work. To understand how illustrators do this, we will start with a description of some of the commonly recognized visual elements of art (table 5.1).

Table 1.   The Visual Elements of Art

Visual Elements of Art	
Line	A continuous point moving from one place to another. May be descriptive (generally define the shape of something), implied (no line is actually present, but a line is created by another visual such as a picket fence), or abstract (nonrepresentational).
Shape	Two-dimensional shape or element
Color	Made up of hue (color), value (degree of lightness), and intensity (level of contrast or strength of color).
Form	Three-dimensional shape or element
Texture	The way the art feels or appears that it would feel
Space	The creation of a depth through the use of proximity of lines and shapes
Perspective	The creation of dimension

How Illustrators Use the Visual Elements of Art

Molly Bang, who is both a writer and a Caldecott Award–winning illustrator of children's books (*When Sophie Gets Angry—Really, Really Angry*, *Ten, Nine, Eight*, and *The Gray Lady and the Strawberry Snatcher*), has provided a useful source for understanding how art in children's books works. Information about Molly's life and work is available at her website: http://www.mollybang.com/main.html

Bang literally takes the elements of art apart in her work so that those of us who are not artists can get a feel for how artists use the elements of art to enhance meaning and evoke emotion. In *Picture This: How Pictures Work*, Bang explores the elements of art and how viewers react to them. Below is a public domain illustration of a fairy tale that will help illustrate Bang's theory.

The compositional elements of color, line, shape, size, space, and contrast make pictures work to convey the story.

1. Color: Of course, *Red Riding Hood*'s cloak is red. Red is often associated with danger. What if *Red Riding Hood*'s cloak were another color, like blue? The trees in the first picture are blue while those in the next two pictures are black or gray. What feeling do the trees evoke? Are the trees in any picture more frightening than the others?

Picture A

Picture B

Picture C

We all recognize the story of *Little Red Riding Hood*.

2. Size: In contrast to *Red Riding Hood*, the wolf is much larger in pictures B and C. Does this make him look more menacing? Bang explains in her book that it does. She explains that larger objects seem more powerful than smaller ones (72).

3. Shape: In picture A, we cannot see the wolf's eye. In picture C, the wolf's eye is slightly triangular. What if the wolf's eye had been an oval? Would it have looked as menacing? What if it had been blue?

4. Line: Bang points out that lines indicate movement. When lines are straight up and down, they are more stable. When they are at angles, they are indicative of movement. In all the pictures, there are several tree limbs at angles. Do they create a sensation of movement and distance? Lines also compare relationship. Compare picture A to pictures B and C. In the first picture, *Red Riding Hood* is some distance from the wolf. It appears that *Red Riding Hood* may even have a chance to get away from the wolf. In picture B, *Red Riding Hood* is deep in the forest with the wolf very near, and in picture C, the wolf has already overtaken her. Which images are more ominous? (46)

5. Space and Contrast: Space adds to depth. In all three pictures, the wolf is fairly close to *Red Riding Hood*. If the wolf were at a greater distance in the background, would he seem as menacing? Contrast in light and dark helps to focus on the main elements as well. For example, notice the contrast between *Red Riding Hood* and her surroundings in picture B. The wolf and the trees are black, and all we see of *Red Riding Hood* is the red cloak and her feet. The wolf is stalking her. Does this contrast help make *Red Riding Hood* look like a target?

The Varied Artistic Styles of Illustrators

Below are examples of artistic styles accessed from the public domain collection of the Metropolitan Museum of Art, New York.

1. *Abstract*: Artwork may not be realistic. The focus is more on evoking mood through the use of lines and abstractions.

   Book Example: *The Noisy Paint Box* by Vasily Kandinsky (has some abstract elements).

Art Example: "House at Dusk" by Georges Seurat

2. *Cartoon*: Somewhat simplified backgrounds with rounded figures, often exaggerated. Understand that the word "cartoon" in art originated during the Renaissance and obviously did not refer to animation as we use the term today. The term meant a large, colorful work of art on board or glass.

Book Example: *Officer Buckle and Gloria* by Peggy Rathmann

Art Example: From *The New York Sunday Journal*. Artist: Ernest Haskell (American, Woodstock, Connecticut 1876–1925 West Point, Maine.)

3. *Cultural*: Art that illustrates a particular culture

Book Example: *The Girl who Loved Wild Horses* by Paul Goble

Art Example: *In Hot Pursuit,* by Charles Schreyvogel

4. *Folk*: Usually set in the past and in rural settings, reflecting the culture of the time in which the story takes place.

    Book Example: *Ox-cart Man* illustrated by Barbara Cooney

Art Example: *Cider Making,* by William Sidney Mount

5. *Impressionistic*: Small, thin, visible brush strokes or pencil lines, emphasize light in various forms, often with very soft lines.

    Book Example: *A Sick Day for Amos McGee* illustrated by Erin E. Stead

Art Example: *Boating,* by Edouard Manet.

6. *Expressionistic*: Usually rich and dramatic, the focus is more on expressing meaning and emotion than on realistic depiction.

   Book Example: *Smoky Night*, Illustrated by David Diaz, Written by Eve Bunting

Art Example: *America Today,* by Thomas Hardy Benton

7. *Realistic*: Seeks to be accurate and true to the real image

   Book Example and Art example: *The Wind in the Willows* by Kenneth Grahame, and illustrated by Graham Robertson

The original book had only one illustration. This book was not a Caldecott winner. There was no Caldecott Medal in 1908 when the book was published, but it is an interesting illustration

8. *Surrealistic*: Dreamlike—often like a bad dream—may have realistic images along with imaginary ones for the purpose of contrast.

Book Example: *The Adventures of Beekle: The Unimaginary Friend*, written and illustrated by Dan Santat

Art Example: *Dreamland*, by S. J. Ferris

A Word about Copyright, Fair Use, and Public Domain

As mentioned earlier, pictures of representative book covers for the various art types are not included in this text. US copyright law is very strict. All published books written prior to 1923 in America are in the public domain. In 2019, the copyright on work published in 1923 will expire, and in 2010, the copyright on work published in 1924 will expire, so the copyright law protects work for seventy-five years. In 1977, copyright law was changed so that anything published after that year either by a single author or multiple authors will not expire until seventy years after the last surviving author dies. Prior to 1964, the law required that work be renewed every twenty-eight years after the initial copyright. If the author failed to renew the copyright, it was lost; thus, a number of books published between 1923 and 1964 have fallen into the public domain owing to failure to renew copyrights, but the only way to be sure is to research the book to determine whether this is the case. Copyright does not protect book or poem titles, nor does it protect facts.

Fair Use in Education Provisions

US copyright law allows for certain **"fair use" of copyrighted material** (particularly important for teachers) if the following four criteria are met:

◆ A: **Purpose of the Use**. Is the copied work to be used in an Education setting or for commercial purposes? Pictures of art works from children's books that are copyrighted may be used in a classroom lesson, but may not be used in this book. Likewise, only poems that fall within the public domain are found in the chapter on poetry.

◆ B: **Nature of the Work**: Only the portions of a work that are relevant to an educational objective may be used. Copies of workbooks and study guides (consumables) which are intended to be purchased by individual students may not be used.

◆ C: **Amount of Work**: Long portions of a work should not be copied. A full journal article or one chapter of a book may be used.

◆ D: **Effect of the Use**: If the use of the work would harm the market for the work itself, the work should not be used. Teachers who use the work of others should provide the source and the copyright information.

In a nutshell, if one uses the guidelines above, it should be clear as to when it is appropriate to use portions of copyrighted works in class.

What Should Teachers Consider When Choosing Illustrated Books for Children?

1. Choose books that are appropriate to the developmental and maturity level of the child. This includes the length of the book and the amount of text. Books that contain some new words and concepts help to deepen the child's critical thinking and comprehension. Very young children will be more interested in the pictures than the text.

2. Choose books that will interest the child so that the child will want to look at them and listen to them.

3. Choose books with illustrations that enhance the content and are true to the story and characters. The styles of the author and illustrator should meld.

4. Choose books that contain interesting pictures that stimulate the child to think more deeply.

5. Choose books that will help the child to understand new concepts or helpful concepts such as sharing and caring.

6. Choose books from a variety of formats including electronic formats so that children are stimulated to look at and interact with the books.

7. Balance book choices so that children are exposed to a number of illustrations that reflect a variety of cultures to help the child expand his or her knowledge of other cultures and ethnicities.

Grammar Review No. 5

Adjectives

Adjectives are words that describe or modify nouns or pronouns in sentences. Three very commonly used adjectives, *a, an,* and *the* are called **articles**.

The <u>pretty</u> girl sat on the <u>dirty</u>, <u>crowded</u> bus. (The underlined words are adjectives.)

Adjectives almost always come directly before the nouns or pronouns they modify. Sometimes, several adjectives in a string come before the nouns or pronouns they modify. Take a look at the example sentence above. Notice that *dirty* and *crowded* are both adjectives. Sometimes, adjectives coming together are divided by a comma, and sometimes they are not. Here is how to tell whether a comma belongs between adjectives or not: If it appears that the word "and" would logically fit between the two adjectives, then a comma is required. In the example above, we could have said that the girl sat on the *dirty and crowded bus*, and that construction would have made sense.

Now, consider another sentence:

At one time, I had a *black Toyota* vehicle. The word *black* describes *vehicle*, not Toyota. The word *Toyota* also describes *vehicle*. We would not be able to insert the word "and" between *black* and *Toyota* and have the sentence make sense. In other words, we would not say that at one time I had a *black and Toyota* vehicle; therefore, no comma belongs between the two adjectives.

Adjectives Have Degrees

The three degrees of adjectives are called the **positive**, **the comparative**, and **the superlative**. Typically, the comparative and superlative forms are made by changing the final letter and adding **er** or **est** to the end of the adjective. The forms of several such adjectives appear in the chart below. These are called regular adjectives.

Positive	Comparative	Superlative
pretty	prettier	prettiest
fat	fatter	fattest
old	older	oldest

Sometimes, the endings of the adjectives do not change in the comparative and superlative forms, but rather, the words *more* or *most* precede the adjectives.

beautiful	more beautiful	most beautiful
annoying	more annoying	most annoying

Finally, some adjectives are irregular, meaning that the word itself changes in the comparative and superlative forms.

good	better	best
bad	worse	worst
little	less	least

Chapter 6

Awards for Children's Books

Alignments

- International Literacy Association: Standard 1
- InTASC, Standards: 2.d, 4.a, 4.l, 4.p, 5r
- ETS, Praxis Exam: 5002 b *Test Specifications*,
- NCTE/CAEP: Standards 1.1, 2.2

Framework

A number of organizations bestow yearly awards for excellence in children's books, and the list is growing. Many of the awards commemorate the work of various figures in the world of children's literature through the centuries. A few of the giants in the genre for whom awards have been named are briefly described in this chapter.

John Newbery (1713–1767) was a British book seller. Newbery established a printshop in London in 1744, one of the first to publish children's books. Newbery published such landmark books for children as *A Little Pretty Pocket Book* and *Little Goody Two Shoes*. The Newbery Medal is probably the oldest and most recognizable award for children's books. Established in 1922, the award commemorates Newbery's contributions to children's literature. (ALSC)

Randolph Caldecott (1846–1886) born in Chester, England, was an author and illustrator of books and other publications. Caldecott's illustrations of children's books were brilliantly colorful and beautiful. He was renowned during his short lifetime for his work. Caldecott wrote (or recounted and illustrated) many nursery rhymes and fables. Among his famous illustrations for children's books are those found in *The House that Jack Built*, *The Babes in the Woods*, and *Sing a Song of Sixpence*. Maurice Sendak wrote of Caldecott: "Caldecott's work heralds the beginning of the modern picture book. He devised an ingenious juxtaposition of picture and word, a counterpoint that never happened before" (Sendak 22).

Theodor Seuss Giesel, also known as Dr. Seuss (1904–1991), was the American grandson of Bavarian immigrants. Born in Springfield, Massachusetts, Giesel graduated from Dartmouth College in 1925. He later did graduate studies at Oxford, but eventually dropped out of graduate school when he realized that he really wanted to draw rather than become a literary scholar. Giesel was a magazine cartoonist in the late 1920s and at that time began signing his name, Dr. Seuss, possibly as a humorous reference to the fact that he dropped out of graduate school. He published his first children's book in 1937, *And to think I saw it all on Mulberry Street*. According to Giesel, somewhere between twenty and twenty-nine publishers turned down his first book. A fortunate encounter with an acquaintance on a street in New York finally lead to its publication. Dr. Seuss was a social and political observer, and spent two years as a political cartoonist for a liberal New York newspaper, *PM*. Some of his children's books drew upon the events of the time, including *Yertle the Turtle*, which mocked the tyrannical reign of Adolph Hitler (Nel). Giesel published forty-five children's books during his lifetime and sold over 650 million. Today, he is known by children everywhere and is one of the most beloved children's authors of all time.

Laura Ingalls Wilder (1867–1957) is an American writer known for the *Little House on the Prairie* books, published from 1942 to 1943. Wilder based her best-selling books on her life as a member of a pioneer family who moved several times between farmsteads in Minnesota, Kansas, Missouri, Dakota Territory, and Indian Territory. Wilder spent a brief period of time as a school teacher, but started her writing career as a newspaper columnist. In 1932, she published her first book, *Little House in the Big Woods*. The book was a success, and she continued writing. In all, Wilder wrote eight books in the *Little House* series, along with a number of others. It is the *Little House* books which are so familiar to American children and for which she gained acclaim. (Laura Ingalls Wilder) Up until June 23, 2018, the Laura Ingalls Wilder Award was given to authors or illustrators who had made a "significant and lasting contribution to children's literature." On that date, the American Library Services for Children (ALSC) voted to strip Wilder's name from the award because, in their words, "This decision was made in consideration of the fact that Wilder's legacy, as represented by her body of work, includes expressions of stereotypical attitudes inconsistent with the ALSC's core values of inclusiveness, integrity and respect, and responsiveness." In other words, Wilder's work has become part of the changing cultural landscape which is rapidly removing references to historical figures whose work or views do not conform to current norms. In general, criticism of Wilder's work suggests that the author's depiction of her family's settlement on the frontier exhibits tones of the "manifest doctrine," which favored white settlement of lands occupied by indigenous peoples. Wilder was the first to win the award in 1954, and it bore her name until 2018.

John Comenius was the author of *Orbis Sensualium Pictus*—**or** *The World of Things Obvious to the Senses Drawn in Pictures*. Published in 1658, this book is considered by many to be the first picture book dedicated to educating children. The book is described in more detail in Chapter 2 of this text. Comenius was an education reformer of some renown. His portrait was painted by Rembrandt, not an honor typically bestowed on just anyone. For his time, he was quite progressive. For example, he advocated for equal educational opportunities for both boys and girls (McNamara).

May Hill Arbuthnot (1884–1969) was an elementary teacher, an administrator, a college professor, and an editor. She coauthored the iconic *Dick and Jane* basal reading series with William Scott Gray, but a greater contribution to children's literature was her textbook, *Children and Books*, published in 1957. Other contributions made by Arbuthnot were here anthologies, *Time for Poetry*, 1951, and *The Arbuthnot Anthology of Children's Literature*, 1953, were an avid advocate of promoting education for children by promulgating a love of reading (Fischer-Wright).

The American Library Association (ALA) provides recognition to contributors to the field of literature and is itself worthy of mention in this chapter. It was founded in 1876 in Philadelphia. The website of the ALA identifies the organization as the "oldest and largest library association in the world." The association identifies its mission as "to provide leadership for the development, promotion and improvement of library and information services and the profession of librarianship in order to enhance learning and ensure access to information for all" (ALA).

Among the ALA's eleven divisions is the **Association of Library Service to Children**, which, again, is the "world's largest organization dedicated to the support and enhancement of library service to children." Some version of the ALSC has been in existence since 1941 when a forerunner or the organization was established as the Division of Libraries for Children and Young People. Today, the ALSC is a very large and active organization that provides numerous services to the public.

The ALSC publishes book lists for children, including yearly summer reading lists and lists of suggested books suitable to be given as gifts. The organization divides suggested books for the following age groups: younger readers (preschool to age 7), middle readers (8–10), older readers (11–14), and all ages. It provides professional development information and e-learning workshops for librarians and educators. The association actively advocates for support for public libraries. It has an active blog, twitter, and wiki presence in addition to the numerous resources available on its extensive website. The ALSC sponsors a number of initiatives including National Drop Everything and Read Day and Children's Book Week (ALSC).

The ALSC is the source of numerous awards for children's books. Below is a listing of these awards. The quoted text in the table below describing the criteria for the awards is taken directly from the ALSC website.

Newbery Winners: Barnes & Noble currently lists the following as their top fifteen best-selling Newbery winners:

1. *A Wrinkle in Time* by Madeleine L'Engle
2. *Hello, Universe* by Erin Entrada Kelly
3. *The One and Only Ivan* by Katherine Applegate
4. *The Giver* by Lois Lowry
5. *The Westing Game* (Puffin ...) by Ellen Raskin
6. *Island of the Blue Dolphins* by Scott O'Dell
7. *The Crossover* by Kwame Alexander
8. *Flora & Ulysses: The Illuminated Adventures* by Kate DiCamillo
9. *Number the Stars* by Lois Lowry
10. *When You Reach Me* by Rebecca Stead

11. *Shiloh* (Shiloh Quartet Series) by Phyllis Reynolds Naylor

12. *The Girl Who Drank the Moon* by Kelly Barnhill

13. *Mrs. Frisby and the Rats of Nihm* by Robert C. O'Brien

14. *Last Stop on Market Street* by Matt de la Peña

15. *Maniac Magee* by Jerry Spinelli

Accessed 24, May 2018, from www.barnesandnoble.com/b/books/newbery-medal/all-newbery-medal-winners/_/N-29Z8q8Z1tna

Table 1. Children's Book Awards

Awards for Children's Books Administered by the American Library Association	
Award	**Awarded to**
The May Hill Arbuthnot Lecture	"an annual event featuring an author, critic, librarian, historian or teacher of children's literature, of any country, who shall prepare a paper considered to be a significant contribution to the field of children's literature."
The Batchelder Award, Est. 1966	"awarded to an American publisher for a children's book considered to be the most outstanding of those books originally published in a foreign language in a foreign country, and subsequently translated into English and published in the United States."
The Pura Belpré Award, Est. 1996	"presented annually to a Latino/Latina writer and illustrator whose work best portrays, affirms, and celebrates the Latino cultural experience in an outstanding work of literature for children and youth."
The Caldecott Medal, Est. 1938	"awarded annually ...to the artist of the most distinguished American picture book for children."
The Geisel (Theodor Seuss) Award, Est. 2006	"given annually to the author(s) and illustrator(s) of the most distinguished American book for beginning readers published in English in the United States during the preceding year."
The Newbery Medal, Est. 1922	"awarded annually by the Association for Library Service to Children, a division of the American Library Association, to the author of the most distinguished contribution to American literature for children."
The Odyssey Award	"jointly given and administered by the Association for Library Service to Children (ALSC) and the Young Adult Library Services Association (YALSA), divisions of ALA, and is sponsored by Booklist magazine." It recognizes the best audio book for children.

Awards for Children's Books Administered by the American Library Association

The Robert F. Sibert Informational Book Medal, Est. 2001	"awarded annually to the author(s) and illustrator(s) of the most distinguished informational book published in the United States in English during the preceding year."
The Children's Literature Legacy Award, formerly The Laura Ingalls Wilder Award, Est. 1954	"honors an author or illustrator whose books, published in the United States, have made, over a period of years, a substantial and lasting contribution to literature for children."
The Schneider Family Book Award	"to honor an author or illustrator for a book that embodies an artistic expression of the disability experience for child and adolescent audiences."

Other Children Book Awards

Award	Awarded by	Awarded to
The NCTE Orbis Pictus Award, Est. 1989	National Council of Teachers of English	"to promote and recognize excellence in the writing of non-fiction for children." (NCTE)
The NCTE Charlotte Huck Award, Est. 2014	National Council of Teachers of English	"recognizes fiction that has the potential to transform children's lives by inviting compassion, imagination, and wonder."(NCTE)
NCTE Award for Excellence in Poetry for Children, Est. 1977	National Council of Teachers of English	"to honor a living American poet for his or her aggregate work for children ages 3-13."(NCTE)
The Coretta Scott King Book Award, Est. 1969	American Library Association and the Coretta Scott King	"given annually to outstanding African American authors and illustrators of books for children and young adults that demonstrate an appreciation of African American culture and universal human values." (ALA)
The CILIP Kate Greenaway Medal, Est. 1955	CILIP: the Chartered Institute of Library and Information Professionals.	"for distinguished illustration in a book for children."(Carnegie-Caldecott Foundation)

Other Children Book Awards		
The American Indian Youth Literature Award, Est. 2006	American Indian Library Association	"established as a way to identify and honor the very best writing and illustrations by and about American Indians. Books selected to receive the award will present American Indians in the fullness of their humanity in the present and past."(AILA)
The Boston Globe Hornbook Awards, Est. 1967	Horn Book Magazine and the Boston Globe	"recognize and reward excellence in literature for children and young adults" https://www.hbook.com/boston-globe-horn-book-awards/bghb-submission-guidelines/. Up to two awards may be bestowed in each of the three following categories: (Boston Globe) ◆ Fiction and Poetry ◆ Nonfiction ◆ Picture Book
The National Book Award for Young People's Literature, Est. 1969	The National Book Foundation	"to recognize the best of American literature, raise the cultural appreciation of great writing, promote the enduring value of reading, and advance the careers of established and emerging" (NBF)
Tom'as Rivera Award	Texas State University	"to honor authors and illustrators who create literature that depicts the Mexican American experience."(TSU)

Other Children Book Awards		
Sydney Taylor Award	Association of Jewish Libraries	"presented annually to outstanding books for children and teens that authentically portray the Jewish experience. Presented by the Association of Jewish Libraries since 1968, the award encourages the publication and widespread use of quality Judaic literature."(AJL)
Americas Book Award	Consortium of Latin Americas Studies Program	"to encourage and commend authors, illustrators and publishers who produce quality children's and young adult books that portray Latin America, the Caribbean, or Latinos in the United States, and to provide teachers with recommendations for classroom use."(CLAS)
Carter G Woodson Award	National Council for the Social Studies	"awarded to the most distinguished social science books appropriate for young readers that depict ethnicity in the United States. The purpose of this award is to encourage the writing, publishing, and dissemination of outstanding social science books for young readers that treat topics related to ethnic minorities and relations sensitively and accurately."(NCSS)

Other Children Book Awards		
Jane Addams Book Award	Jane Addams Peace Association	"annually recognizes children's books of literary and aesthetic excellence that effectively engage children in thinking about peace, social justice, global community, and equity for all people." (Jane Addams Peace Foundation)
The Hans Christian Andersen Award (two awards)	IBBY-The International Board on Books for Young People	"recognize lifelong achievement and are presented to an author and an illustrator whose complete works have made an important, lasting contribution to children's literature."(IBBY)

Caldecott Winners: Barnes & Noble currently lists the following as their top fifteen best-selling Caldecott winners:

1. *Where the Wild Things Are* by Maurice Sendak

2. *Wolf in the Snow* by Matthew Cordell

3. *Finding Winnie: The True Story of the World's Most Famous Bear* by Lindsay Mattick

4. *Make way for Ducklings* by Robert McCloskey

5. *The Snowy Day* by Ezra Jack Keats

6. *The Adventures of Beekle: The Unimaginary Friend* by Dan Santat

7. *Owl Moon* by Jane Yolen

8. *The Invention of Hugo Cabret* by Brian Selznick

9. *Kitten's First Full Moon* by Kevin Henkes

10. *Sylvester and the Magic Pebble* by William Steig

11. *Radiant Child: The Story of Young Artist Jean-Michel Basquiat* by Javaka Steptoe

12. *Snowflake Bentley* by Jacqueline Briggs Martin, illustrated by Mary Azarian

13. *The Girl Who Loved Wild Horses* by Paul Goble

14. *This Is Not My Hat* by Jon Klassen

15. *Officer Buckle and Gloria* by Peggy Rathmann

Accessed 24 May, 2018, from www.barnesandnoble.com/b/books/caldecott-medal/all-caldecott-medal-winners/_/N-29Z8q8Z1sb1

What Should Teachers Consider When Selecting Award-Winning Books for Children?

1. Choose books that are appropriate to the developmental and maturity level of the child. Books that contain some new words and concepts help to deepen the child's critical thinking and comprehension. This includes the length of the book and the amount of text.

2. Choose books that will stimulate the child's interest and that the child will want to read or have read to him or her so that the child's interest in reading is increased by the experience.

3. Remember that award-winning books are almost always selected by committees whose members are well versed in the review of children's literature and who are guided by a set criterion in the selection. It is unlikely that any books have been chosen that do not meet the criteria.

4. Remember that there is some merit in most award-winning books.

5. Be aware that award-winning books are popular books, and therefore may be books that children are familiar with or have heard of. This can help pique the child's interest in the book.

6. Choose books that will help the child to understand new concepts or helpful concepts such as sharing and caring.

7. Choose books from a variety of formats including electronic formats so that children are stimulated to look at and interact with the books.

8. Balance book choices so that children are exposed to a number of illustrations that reflect a variety of cultures to help them expand their knowledge of other cultures and ethnicities.

9. Do not automatically assume that because a book has won an award it is suitable for classroom use. Consider the topics and how they fit into the curriculum as well as the values of the school and the community.

The following are some well known Award-Winning Illustrators (with one example book)

Barbara Cooney, *Miss Rumphius*

Leo and Diane Dillon, *Why Mosquitos Buzz in People's Ears* (African art)

Robert McCloskey, *Make Way for Ducklings* (has sold more than two million copies)

Chris Van Allsburg, *The Polar Express*

David Wiesner, *Tuesday* (example of surrealism)

Grammar Review No. 6

Adverbs

An adverb is a word that modifies an adjective, verb, or another adverb. They often end in *ly*, and they usually tell *which one, what kind, how many, how much, or under what conditions* about the words they modify.

Examples:

1. She ran *frantically* to the car. (Adverb: *frantically*, modifying the verb, *ran*.)

2. They have a *very* beautiful house. (Adverb: *very*, modifying the adjective: *beautiful*.)

3. The book was *quite* literally beyond my comprehension. (Adverb: *quite*, modifying another adverb: *literally*.)

Adverbs Have Forms

Just as adjectives have comparative and superlative forms, adverbs can have them as well.

4. Study *hard* if you want to pass the test. (Adverb *hard*, modifying the verb: *study*.)

5. Study *harder* if you want to pass the test. (*Comparative* form of adverb, *harder*, modifying the verb: *study*.)

6. Study *hardest* if you want to make the highest score in the class. (Superlative form of adverb, modifying the verb: *study*.)

When a phrase or a clause acts as an adverb in a sentence, it is an adverbial phrase or an adverbial clause.

Conjunctive adverbs are described in the Grammar Review No. 7.

Chapter 7

Contemporary and Multicultural Children's Literature

Alignments

- International Literacy Association: Standard 1
- InTASC, Standards: 2d, 2k,2m, 4.a, 4.l, 4.p, 5e
- ETS, Praxis Exam: 5002 b *Test Specifications*,
- NCTE/CAEP: Standards 1.1, 2.2

Framework

Contemporary children's literature can be distinguished from traditional children's literature in that contemporary literature was written by a known author. Older stories that derived from the oral tradition, even though in print, are classified as traditional books if there is no known author. This chapter provides a background and general description of contemporary children's literature and will explore multicultural literature for classroom use as well.

Contemporary literature now contains numerous books that depict multiculturalism. We will define multicultural children's literature as literature that has as primary characters persons who belong to one of the American ethnicities or cultural groups such as African American, Latino, Hispanic, Native American, Asian Americans, Jewish, Indian Americans, and others, or that relates stories and information about the native lands and cultures of these groups or their ancestors. Literature that focuses on girls and women as well as persons with disabilities and persons from regions of America that are not considered mainstream are also included as part of the multicultural tapestry. We will explore literature from the various genres and provide information about a few specific selections. Readers will not find, in this chapter, a review of literature that contains a political or social agenda or seeks to portray any race or group in any stereotypical fashion. Readers will find, in this chapter, a review of multicultural literature that supports its use as a means of promoting cultural understanding and broadens the education of children of all races and cultural groups.

The Popularity of Contemporary Children's Literature

There is no doubt that contemporary children's and young adult's literature is a big business. Witness the enormous success of the *Harry Potter Series*, the *Hunger Games Series*, the *Twilight Series*, the *Lord of the Rings Series*, the *Narnia Series*, the *Sisterhood Series*, and the list goes on.

In an edited version of a speech made in aid of Belsize Park Library in 2015, entitled *Why This Is a Golden Age for Children's Literature, Children's Books Are One of the Most Important Forms of Writing We Have*, Amanda Craig, British book reviewer, posits that we are living in the third golden age of children's literature. Craig points out the current success of children's literature as a genre and names writers such as J. K. Rowling, David Williams, and John Green, all of whom have earned millions for their publishers, as exemplary authors of this genre in this golden age.

Craig describes two previous golden ages. She describes the first golden age as that which began in the 1850s and was dominated by such writers as J. M. Barrie (*Peter Pan*), Robert Louis Stevenson (*Treasure Island*), E. Nesbit (*The Story of the Treasure Seekers*, *The Wouldbegoods*, *The Revolt of the Toys*), Frances Hodgson Burnett (*Little Lord Fauntleroy*, *The Secret Garden*), and Anna Sewell (*Black Beauty*). Craig also notes that the children in the books of the first golden age tended to act rather than contemplate and that books tended to focus on what we would call traditional values such as duty and self-sacrifice (Craig).

The second golden age occurred after World War II and continued until the 1970s. It provided the young literature read by the baby boomers. The literature of this age took a dark tone and focused on the global struggle between good and evil. It was during this era that Roald Dahl (*James and the Giant Peach*, *Charlie and the Chocolate Factory*, *Matilda*), Judith Kerr (*The Mog* series of picture books for young children and acclaimed books for older children such as *When Hitler Stole Pink Rabbit*), and Maurice Sendak (*Where the Wild Things Are*) became so popular. Fantasy was a very popular genre. It was in the 1950s that Tolkien published *Lord of the Rings* and his close friend, C. S. Lewis published his seven-book *Narnia* series (Craig).

In an article in *Publisher's Weekly*, entitled "New Trends in YA, The Agent's Perspective," Sue Corbett notes some interesting trends in the world of young adult literature. Corbett provides snippets from interviews with publishers. For example, Josh Adams of Adams Literary indicates that some of the themes in young adult literature are shifting. Postapocalyptic stories and stories that include love triangles involving the paranormal are waning. Likewise, books about dystopia (ala *The Hunger Games* and *Divergent*) are also playing out. What is on the uptick? Michael Bourret of Dystel and Goderich Literary Management indicates that the evolving field today is that of Realistic Fiction and points to the success of authors such as John Greene (*The Fault in our Stars*) and Rainbow Rowell's *Eleanor and Park*. Vampires and werewolves may have seen their day for a while. Thrillers like *Suicide Notes*, later sold in movie form as *Gone Girl*, are popular now (Corbett).

In reference to the popularity of young adult literature, Corbett noted that a slight majority of submissions, at least to some publishers, is of the YA genre. A cursory Google search of the most popular genres today is likely to reveal that romance novels are the top sellers in America. Keep in mind that the classification of books into the romance genre is broad and can include everything from good literature to the—well, not so good. Some data sources include young adult romance novels in the overall genre of romance (Corbett).

New Literacies

During the 1990s, a group of ten academics, primarily from the United States, the UK, and Australia met in New London, New Hampshire, to review the way English is taught globally and to make recommendations as to how the teaching of English should be changed to meet the needs of a changing world. To oversimplify, the group advocated a focus on teaching multicultural English as it has evolved rather than teaching competencies in a standardized form of English as it has been taught for centuries. That concept didn't catch on, and the group's suggestions will not be addressed here. The group had a second focus on the concept of multiliteracies as they pertain to the changes that technology has brought to the world of literacy (The New London Group 60). In this regard, with changes including texting, e-mail, social media, entertainment media, e-books, and many others that emerge almost daily, we could agree that multiliteracy is a necessary tool in the twenty-first century.

The sheer number of available instructional websites and aps for teachers and children is overwhelming. Some free websites for teachers of children's literature are listed at the end of selected chapters in this book. There are many, many more that are interactive and that children may find exciting. Children live in a world dominated by the use of ever-changing technology, and they are savvy. Classroom instruction must incorporate at least some technology in order to keep children engaged. The Association for Library Service to Children (ALSC) now provides a list of Notable Children's Digital Media. The 2018 annotated list contains eighteen Android and IOS aps that are recommended for instructional use. To illustrate how quickly the digital world is evolving, the committee that selects the aps for this list was called the Great Websites Committee until 2017; they have evolved to the review of aps instead. This list can be accessed at http://www.ala.org/alsc/awardsgrants/notalists/ncdm.

Teachers should keep in mind that technology is not a substitute for the teacher. Indeed, many classroom teachers with whom we are acquainted express some trepidation at what they see as the overuse of technology to the point that teacher and student engagement may be diminished and learning may actually be impaired. The goal is to incorporate technology into the curriculum, not to use technology for technology's sake.

Multicultural Literature and Why It Is Important

Consider this: For centuries in Europe, and later in America, parents who could afford to do so have sent their children abroad after graduating college. This practice even had a name, "The Grand Tour." The purpose of the trip was to absorb the aesthetics of other cultures. James Boswell (1740–1795) attributes the following quote to Samuel Johnson: "A man who has not been in Italy is always conscious of an inferiority, from his not having seen what it is expected a man should see." (Boswell). Granted, far more young men than women were afforded this opportunity, and the destinations were primarily European, in no small part because worldwide transportation was not readily available to other continents; nevertheless, the practice itself demonstrates the importance that people have traditionally placed on experiencing other cultures. Today, the practice of educational travel continues through college tours and of course through private travel. Travel is possible to almost any place on the planet, and many colleges and universities now offer study abroad opportunities all over the world, depending upon the course or educational discipline with which the trip is aligned.

Consider also that human society is now a global society. Technology and international economic trade have made this a reality. Additionally, in the United States, society has become very diverse. Persons of all ethnicities and from all over the world are American citizens. We have at our disposal, in our schools, the opportunity to provide our students with a rich education, one that involves knowledge and understanding of cultures other than their own, and the primary resource for this opportunity is students themselves.

What Does It Mean to Be Culturally Sensitive?

In its most basic sense, cultural sensitivity means an awareness and an appreciation of characteristics of other persons. To be culturally sensitive, we must be culturally aware, accept the obvious fact that differences exist in people and strive to assign no value to one culture over another. While pride in one's own culture need not be discouraged in any group, all groups must be willing to be self-reflective of their own cultures and any possible biases they may have about others.

What Does the Culturally Sensitive Language Arts Classroom Look Like?

In a culturally sensitive language arts classroom, the teacher makes an impact on the climate by modeling the following:

1. Showing genuine respect for other cultures, languages, and traditions by including them in instruction in a natural way. For example, when teaching a reading concept, intermittently select multicultural picture books that enhance the concept being taught.

2. Learning to pronounce names correctly, and seeing that students do the same thing.

3. Speaking slowly and clearly, particularly to English-language learners.

4. Taking time to listen carefully when students of other cultures want to share about their cultures or homelands.

5. Demonstrating interest in other cultures, and showing that learning about them has educational value.

The Controversy over Selecting Multicultural Literature for the Classroom

Awareness and acknowledgement of the need for cultural sensitivity is the prerequisite for incorporating multicultural children's literature in classroom instruction and activities. In fact, that is the easy part. Then comes the determination of the literature to be used and the necessity of using multicultural, and in fact all literature, appropriately—as a natural component of the instruction rather than an element that is just inserted for the sake of covering a base. In America today, multiculturalism itself is a heated political topic, and if elementary teachers are to make a real contribution to the societal futures of the children in our classrooms, we might consider teaching in a way that is nonpolitical and nonjudgmental. In other words, we might focus on including literature that fosters appreciation of others rather than historical or social criticism.

What Should Be Considered When Selecting Multicultural Children's Literature?

Not surprisingly, most of the same criteria apply to the selection of multicultural children's literature that apply to selecting any literature.

1. **Authority:** This is a topic of serious debate and can be quite political. Authority refers to the authenticity of the author. There is a school of thought that argues that only a person of a particular ethnicity is capable of or has the "authority" to write about that ethnicity. In fact, some suggest that members of minority groups do not always "trust people whom they identify as members of the oppressing group to tell their stories" and that African American literature, for example, is only African American if it has been written by an African American (Bishop 16). Others may suggest that writing stories about a different ethnicity does not differ from writing about other topics which one has carefully researched or with which one has close ties (Wilfong). This argument applies to all ethnicities. For example, can an African American write about white American culture? Can a white American write about China, its people and customs? Pearl Buck did so in 1931 after living in China for some time. The title of the novel was *The Good Earth*. It won the Pulitzer Prize in 1932, and, as the first in a trilogy, it was influential in Buck's being awarded the Nobel Prize for Literature in 1938. This text will take no stance as to which argument is correct. The selection of literature, in most cases, is up to the good judgment of the aware and reflective teacher. The teacher who is true to the tenets of respect for all cultures and carefully reviews the books that he or she is considering will make good choices.

2. **Setting:** Teachers should select works that feature more than one traditional setting for multicultural literature. It is certainly important to select literature that helps enlighten all students on the historical and traditional origins of various cultures, but it is a new world, and the lives of all ethnicities, while retaining many traditions, have also evolved. For example, African American stories do not always have to be tied to the continent of Africa, nor do they always have to be tied to urban settings in America. African Americans are part of all walks of life in society; therefore, teachers should look for authentic stories in a variety of settings. Recall that Ezra Jack Keats' landmark *The Snowy Day* takes place in a city and centers on a young African American boy who is just a typical boy who lives in an apartment and loves playing in the snow like any other typical boy.

    Likewise, Native American stories need not always depict the Plains Indians of the 1800s or similar settings. Although most Native Americans do live in western states, many also live in the great urban centers, with Los Angeles and New York having the greatest concentration of city dwellers (U.S. Census Bureau). While stories of the historical and traditional experience of Native American peoples are the legitimate focus of most Native American children's literature and might constitute the majority of classroom selections, stories of the contemporary Native American experience should be included as well. Joseph Bruchac has written a number of such stories, including a fairly recent chapter book for ages 6–10 entitled *Eagle Song*. This story depicts the struggle of a young boy who is trying to reconcile two cultures. The point is that multicultural literature chosen for the classroom should avoid stereotypes and present a broad, realistic, and authentic view of culture, from the traditional to the modern world.

3. **Style:** The author's style should, again, be authentic, realistic, and free from exaggerations. For example, stories about Appalachian children should not reflect the stereotype of the rural, the uneducated, the backward, and the poor. Consider that several major urbanized areas exist in Appalachia, among them Pittsburgh, Asheville, Knoxville, Chattanooga, and Birmingham. Again, children from this region are like children everywhere. Appalachians have a rich and proud heritage that is now depicted in many stories such as, *When I Was Young in the Mountains*, by Cynthia Rylant.

4. **Characters:** The characters are individuals, not group stereotypes. Look for books that contain all kinds of diversity, including persons with disabilities portrayed as people, not representatives of disability groups.

An Essential Book for Language Arts Teachers

The Norton Anthology of Children's Literature: The Tradition in English: editors, Jack Zipes, Lisa Paul, Lynne Vallone, Peter Hunt, and Gillian Avery. Published by W. W. Norton and Company, 2005.

This book is a veritable encyclopedia of children's and young adult literature and literary criticism. It contains information about, excerpts from, or the complete works of virtually all major contributions to English children's literature since 1659. It includes prose, poetry, drama, and all their subgenres. It is a must-have.

Free Internet Resources for Teachers

http://hca.gilead.org.il/#list Hans Christian Andersen, Fairy Tales and Stories. This website contains almost all we ever want to know about Hans Christian Andersen and contains all his stories.

www.storyarts.org Story Arts Online. This website contains the texts of hundreds of folktales and stories, including Aesop's fables. It also contains audio recordings of stories. Multicultural works are included.

www.pitt.edu/~dash/folktexts.html This website contains the texts of hundreds, possibly more than a thousand, stories, separated by genre. It is maintained by D. L. Ashlamin at the University of Pittsburgh. It is not a site for children to use on their own because there are no pictures, and some of the stories could be disturbing to young children. For example, there is a section of anti-Semitic folktales from Europe. There are tales from many countries which makes this an excellent source for multicultural stories.

https://www.edutopia.org/blog/integrating-technology-and-literacy-frank-ward this is a free website maintained by Frank Ward, a teacher, who has compiled a number of useful ways to include technology in the language arts curriculum.

Grammar Review No. 7

Conjunctions and Interjections

A conjunction is a word used to connect words, phrases, or clauses in a sentence. A conjunction is a joiner. As with all of the other parts of speech, there are different kinds of conjunctions.

Coordinating Conjunctions Also Known As, the FANBOYS

For, and, nor, but, or, yet, so

These are the simplest conjunctions, and their function is the simplest as well.

They connect *words* as in

1. Mary loves chocolate *and* vanilla equally.

   They connect *clauses* as in

2. Mary loves chocolate ice cream, *but* she loves vanilla ice cream more.

3. They can also connect phrases or a string of phrases.

   What are clauses? A clause is a group of words that contains a subject and its verb. They come in two types: **independent** and **dependent** (**also called subordinate**).

   In sentence 2, there are two *independent* clauses. An **independent clause can stand alone as a complete sentence**.

   Mary loves chocolate ice cream is a complete sentence.

   She loves vanilla ice cream more is also a complete sentence.

   These two independent clauses are joined by the conjunction, *but*. When you join independent clauses with a conjunction, you place a comma in front of the conjunction. (*Note: There are times when it is alright to omit the comma, but there are never times when the comma is incorrect*, so the suggestion here is to always use the comma.)

   Now let's look at dependent (or subordinate) clauses.

4. Because Mary loves ice cream so much, she allows herself to indulge only once per week.

   This sentence contains a dependent (subordinate) clause: *because Mary loves ice cream so much*

   This clause has a subject, *Mary*, and a verb, *loves*, but it does not express a complete thought; therefore, it is not a complete sentence. When a dependent clause *precedes* an independent clause in a sentence, *the clauses are separated by a comma*. Note the comma placement in the sentence above. Now, look at sentence 4.

5. Mary allows herself to indulge in ice cream only once per week because she loves it so much.

   When a dependent clause *follows* an independent clause, *no comma is used to separate them*.

   Should you begin a sentence with a coordinating conjunction?

Grammar purists will say no, but there are times when beginning a sentence with a conjunction adds effect to what you are trying to say. See the example below.

In the beginning of April, the trenches were filled with rain at the western front, and it got worse.

In the beginning of April, the trenches were filled with rain at the western front. And it got worse.

Notice that the second sentence is a little more dramatic. The point is that you can start a sentence with a coordinating conjunction if it enhances the writing.

Subordinating Conjunctions

after	before	so that
although	even though	though
as	if	unless
as if	now that	until
as long as	once	when
as though	rather than	whenever
because	since	whereas

The chart shows several of the subordinating conjunctions. There are many others. Subordinating conjunctions make one clause *subordinate or dependent on another*. Look at sentence 3 again.

Because Mary loves ice cream so much, she allows herself to indulge only once per week.

This sentence begins with a subordinating conjunction. Because it begins with a subordinating conjunction, the first clause is a subordinate clause. It depends on another clause to complete its meaning. If we remove the subordinating conjunction, the clause would become an independent clause as shown below.

Mary loves ice cream so much.

As with previous examples, subordinating conjunctions can appear anywhere in the sentence; they do not have to begin the sentence. Refer to sentence 4 for an example.

Correlative Conjunctions

These are just conjunctions that are used in pairs.

neither/nor, both/and, if/then, not only/but also, either/or

Conjunctive Adverbs

Conjunctive adverbs are not exactly conjunctions, but they are joiners. *They join two independent clauses in sentences.*

Examples: however, therefore, nevertheless, moreover, nonetheless, conversely, furthermore, thus, instead, indeed.

The main thing to remember about conjunctive adverbs is how to punctuate them. Conjunctive adverbs are separated from the independent clauses by *both a semicolon and a comma*.

6. Mary tries to limit her ice cream **intake; nevertheless, she** eats it all the time.

Notice in sentence 5 that the conjunctive adverb, *nevertheless*, is separated by both a semicolon and a conjunction. There are two correlative conjunctions in that sentence as well. Can you find them?

Interjections

Interjections are by far the easiest parts of speech to remember. They are simply words that express emotion, surprise, or just make a point. They are usually used at the beginning of a sentence, but are sometimes used alone. They are often, but not always followed by exclamation points. Practically any other part of speech can be used as an interjection.

Examples: Excuse me, Oh! Good Excellent, Well! No! Hello, Goodbye

Chapter 8

Prose

Alignments

- International Literacy Association: Standard 1
- InTASC, Standards: 4.f, 4.k, 4.l
- ETS, Praxis Exam: 5002 b *Test Specifications*,
- NCTE/CAEP: Standards 1.1, 2.2

Framework

In Chapter 3, we learned about genre in literature. As was true with the previous exploration of genre, a listing of genre in children's literature is also hard to nail down. Even a cursory review of sources demonstrates that the categories or genres in children's literature are varied, and indeed, seem to depend largely on the opinions of the source writers. For our purposes, we will retain the two major categories of Prose and Poetry as we attempt to classify children's literature, although many consider Poetry a form rather than a genre. This chapter focuses on the myriad of forms found in prose for children and young adults.

Prose Formats

Picture Books: These books typically appeal to younger children. The text and the pictures are intertwined. These books can come in any genre. Example: *Where the Wild Things Are* by Maurice Sendak.

First Books: Books for infants and very young children. Designed to introduce the child to the world and to hold up to play and exploration. Often made of cloth, cardboard, or plastic. Example: *Ten Little Fingers and Ten Little Toes* by Mem Fox, illustrated by Helen Oxenbury.

Toy Books: Became popular during the Victorian era. Can be made of cloth, cardboard, or plastic, and tend to be durable. Mechanical in some way. Includes pop-up books, books with sliding cardboard tabs and similar constructions. More art than literature.

Rhythmic Books: Have a rhyming or musical quality. Examples: *Yertle the Turtle* by Dr. Seuss and nursery rhymes. The rhyming helps increase a child's vocabulary and develop **phonological awareness**.

Chapter Books: As the name implies, fiction written in chapters for younger readers (up to about the age of 12.)

Concept Books: Storybooks that teach a lesson or a concept. The book may or may not have a plot. The focus is on the lesson to be learned, and that can be anything from cleaning a room to a science or social skills lesson. Example: *Eat Your Colors* by Amanda Miller.

Graphic Novels: These books generally appeal to older children and adolescents because they assist students in visualizing the plot and they help readers to see the tone of the dialogue. They are sometimes confused with comic books, but they are somewhat different. Like comic books, graphic novels use picture frames to tell the story, but they are more likely to involve complex characters and plots. Example: *Watchmen Series* by Alan Moore, illustrated by Dave Gibbons, colorist: John Higgins.

Prose Types		
Fiction contains one or more elements that does not conform to the laws of our universe **Traditional Prose is anything for which there is no known author**.		*Nonfiction* must contain things as they are in our physical universe. No elements that do not fit this description can be included.
Contemporary Realistic Fiction (conforms to the laws of the universe) **A. Historical Fiction** (takes place in the past). Example: *Fallen Angels* by William Dean Myers	*Contemporary Fantasy Fiction* (has at least one element that does not conform to the laws of the universe) **1. Traditional Fantasy** (old stories that began with oral tradition and have no identifiable author)	A. Biography B. Informational C. Concept Books D. Issue Books E. Authentic Journals F. Newspapers

Prose Types		
B. YA, Young Adult Fiction *Subgenres* School Stories Coming of Age Stories Mystery Dystopia Paranormal Romance	**2. Folklore,** the entire category of artistic expression of a culture, includes folktales **3. Cumulative Tales,** Cumulative sentences and actions are repeated throughout. Every time a new action occurs, the previous actions that lead up to it must be repeated. Example: *There Was an Old Lady Who Swallowed a Fly.* **4. Pourquoi,** tales that explain how things came to be the way they are. Example: "How the Leopard Got His Spots."	

Contemporary Realistic Fiction	Contemporary Fantasy Fiction	Nonfiction
Graphic Novels Horror Adventure Chick Lit	**1.** Tall Tales, folk stories that grossly exaggerate folk heroes. Example: *Paul Bunyan*. **2.** Fairy tales—always end happily **3.** Fables, short simple stories that teach lessons. Example: *Aesop's Fables*. **4.** Parables, stories that illustrate a truth by providing a scenario. Example: The parables of the Bible. **5.** Myths, contain gods or the supernatural; generally explain the origin of something. **6.** Legends, heroic tales, highly embellished **7. YA, Young Adult Fiction,** the subgenres listed in column 1, written for older children. **B.** Modern Fantasy, has an identifiable author and has therefore appeared in print. Example: *Harry Potter* **1.** Science Fiction, Example: *Ender's Game*	

Considerations about Prose

Most classroom text is prose, and it is used for a variety of purposes. One purpose for using books in the classroom is for vocational reading, or for learning to read. Picture books and chapter books abound at every reading level. Teachers can select books that interest children as they build reading skills or that will supplement the skills learned in a Basal reader.

Another purpose is to use books at appropriate reading levels to enhance content in other areas of the curriculum. Indeed, this is an expectation of the Common Core Standards, and remember, most states use these standards or a version of them. A third reason is for aesthetic reading, or what Elizabeth Gruner describes as a cultivated appreciation of literature (Gruner). In the selection of books for this purpose, teachers should pay particular attention to the interests of children and then build on and broaden the child's tastes in literature. This is the highest purpose of reading, reading for enrichment, and it, too should be nurtured.

Chapter 9

Poetry

"Poetry is language at its most distilled and most powerful."
- Rita Dove

Alignments

▶ International Literacy Association: Standard 1
▶ InTASC, Standards: 1g, 2d, 4.l, 4.p
▶ ETS, Praxis Exam: 5002 b *Test Specifications*
▶ NCTE/CAEP: Standards 1.1, 2.2

Framework

Ah, poetry. It is often neglected in the classroom, generally for three reasons: (1) The teacher may not personally like poetry because he or she did not have a good experience with poetry while in school. (2) The teacher may not feel that he or she knows enough about poetry to really teach it. (3) The children may enjoy rhythmic poems and music, but may be intimidated by the study of poetry and its concepts in the later grades. We cannot let any of these excuses prevent us from exposing children to the enjoyment of poetry. We have already reviewed many literary devices in Chapter 3. This chapter focuses on the structural elements of poetry and the forms and types of poems enjoyed by children and young adults.

Elements of Poetry
Structural Elements

1. **Line**: A row of words in a poem

2. **Stanza**: A series of lines separated by an empty line (no text)

Types of stanzas	
Couplet: two lines	dos lines
Tercet: three lines	tres lines
Quatrain: four lines	cuatro lines
Cinquain: five lines	cinco lines
Sestet: six lines	seis lines
Septet: seven lines	siete lines
Octave: eight lines	ocho lines

(Teaching Tip: Combine teaching the definitions for number of lines in a stanza *with counting in Spanish*. Most of the words are similar, as shown above, and it is a good way to incorporate multiculturalism.)

3. **Rhyme**: Repetition of similar sounds. This may or may not be present in a poem.

4. **End rhyme**: Occurs at the end of succeeding lines

5. **Internal rhyme**: Occurs in the middle of succeeding lines

6. **Rhyme scheme**: The pattern of ending rhyme in lines of poetry. It is marked by letters and is done by stanzas. The sound at the end of the first line of a stanza is designated by the letter A, the second sound by the letter B, and so on. Successive stanzas continue the pattern. Each time the same sound is repeated, it is designated by the letter assigned to it when it first appeared at the end of a line in the poem.

Example of AABBA rhyme scheme:

Twinkle, twinkle little star (A)

How I wonder what you are (A)

Up above the world so high (B)

Like a diamond in the sky (B)

How I wonder what you are (A)

Rhyme Scheme, longer example:
Paul Revere's Ride by Henry Wadsworth Longfellow

Listen, my children, and you shall hear (A)

Of the midnight ride of Paul Revere, (A)

On the eighteenth of April, in Seventy-five (B)

Hardly a man is now alive (B)

Who remembers that famous day and year.(A)

He said to his friend, "If the British march (C)

By land or sea from the town to-night,(D)

Hang a lantern aloft in the belfry arch (C)

Of the North Church tower as a signal light—(D)

One, if by land, and two, if by sea; (E)

And I on the opposite shore will be, (E)

Ready to ride and spread the alarm (F)

Through every Middlesex village and farm (F)

For the country folk to be up and to arm." (F)

Common Rhyme Schemes

    A. Alternate Rhyme is probably the most common rhyme scheme. ABAB

    B. Monorhyme is also very common. AAAA

    C. Enclosed Rhyme: ABBA

    D. Rhyming Couplets: AA, BB, CC, and so on

    E. **Slant Rhyme**: can be difficult to define or recognize, because the words *don't really rhyme*. The words at the end of lines may have either the same consonant ending consonant: *cat, pet* or the same vowel sound in the last syllable: *cat, mad*

  7. **Rhythm**: The pattern of stressed and unstressed syllables in a line. The beat of a poem. It results from the meter. (Think of music and any Dr. Seuss poem.)

(Note: We have never found a satisfactory definition to distinguish between rhythm and meter. They are very closely related.)

  1. **Meter**: A repetitive rhythm. Meter determines rhythm

  2. **Feet or foot**: The building blocks of meter

Types of metric feet—determined by the number of stressed and unstressed syllables in a unit

    A. Iamb: unstressed/stressed   Example words: remove, exist, we played

    B. Trochee: stressed/unstressed   Example words: raven, double, people

    C. Spondee: stressed/stressed   Example words: downtown, doorway, sunshine

    D. Anapest: unstressed/unstressed/stressed   Example words: interrupt, comprehend

    E. Dactyl: stressed/unstressed/unstressed   Example words: typical, fabulous

(Teaching Tip: Pneumonic device for helping students to remember the types of metric feet: Remember the word ITSAD (short for: It's sad) to help students remember the first letters of the five types of feet: Iamb, Trochee, Spondee, Anapest, and Dactyl.)

Structural Forms

1. *Acrostic*: a name poem

The letters of the name are written vertically. Then a word, phrase, or sentence that begins with each letter is added. It is not necessary that the name be that of a person. Some acrostic poems are written about things such as SUMMER or other nouns.

Example: Edgar Allan Poe's *An Acrostic* (public domain)

Elizabeth it is in vain you say

"Love not"-thou sayest it in so sweet a way:

In vain those words from thee or L.E.L.

Zantippe's talents had enforced so well:

Ah! if that language from thy heart arise,

Breath it less gently forth-and veil thine eyes.

Endymion, recollect, when Luna tried

To cure his love-was cured of all beside-

His follie-pride-and passion-for he died.

2. *Alphabet Poem*: each line begins with a successive letter.

Alphabet Poem Example: The following is Edward Lear's (1812–1888) nonsense alphabet poem (public domain). Note that this poem contains words that will be new to most children and thus grow their vocabularies. Examples: sugar tongs, yew, urn, zinc

A was an ant
Who seldom stood still,
And who made a nice house
In the side of a hill.
a!
Nice little ant!

B was a book
With a binding of blue,
And pictures and stories
For me and for you.
b!
Nice little book!

C was a cat
Who ran after a rat;
But his courage did fail
When she seized on his tail.
c!
Crafty old cat!

D was a duck
With spots on his back,
Who lived in the water,
And always said "Quack!"
d!
Dear little duck!

E was an elephant,
Stately and wise:
He had tusks and a trunk,
And two queer little eyes.
e!
Oh, what funny small eyes!

F was a fish
Who was caught in a net;
But he got out again,
And is quite alive yet.
f!
Lively young fish!

G was a goat
Who was spotted with brown:
When he did not lie still
He walked up and down.
g!
Good little goat!

H was a hat
Which was all on one side;
Its crown was too high,
And its brim was too wide.
h!
Oh, what a hat!

I was some ice
So white and so nice,
But which nobody tasted;
And so it was wasted.
i!
All that good ice!

J was a jackdaw
Who hopped up and down
In the principal street
Of a neighboring town.
j!
All through the town!

K was a kite
Which flew out of sight,
Above houses so high,
Quite into the sky.
k
Fly away, kite!

L was a light
Which burned all the night,
And lighted the gloom
Of a very dark room.
l!
Useful nice light!

M was a mill
Which stood on a hill,
And turned round and
round
With a loud hummy sound.
m!
Useful old mill!

N was a net
Which was thrown in
the sea
To catch fish for dinner
For you and for me.
n!
Nice little net!

O was an orange
So yellow and round:
When it fell off the tree,
It fell down to the ground.
o!
Down to the ground!

P was a pig,
Who was not very big;
But his tail was too curly,
And that made him surly.
p!
Cross little pig!

Q was a quail
With a very short tail;
And he fed upon corn
In the evening and morn.
q!
Quaint little quail!

R was a rabbit,
Who had a bad habit
Of eating the flowers
In gardens and bowers.
r!
Naughty fat rabbit!

S was the sugar-tongs,
Nippity-nee,
To take up the sugar
To put in our tea.
s!
Nippity-nee!

T was a tortoise,
All yellow and black:
He walked slowly away,
And he never came back.
t!
Torty never came back!

U was an urn
All polished and bright,
And full of hot water
At noon and at night.
u!
Useful old urn!

V was a villa
Which stood on a hill,
By the side of a river,
And close to a mill.
v!
Nice little villa!

W was a whale
With a very long tail,
Whose movements were frantic
Across the Atlantic.
w!
Monstrous old whale!

X was King Xerxes,
Who, more than all Turks, is
Renowned for his fashion
Of fury and passion.
x!
Angry old Xerxes!

Y was a yew,
Which flourished and grew
By a quiet abode
Near the side of a road.
y!
Dark little yew!

Z was some zinc,
So shiny and bright,
Which caused you to wink
In the sun's merry light.
z!
Beautiful zinc!

3. *Human **Haiku**/Senryu*: A poem of three lines in the modern American Version. Traditional Japanese Haiku poems were quite differently constructed and were longer.

Five syllables

Seven syllables

Five syllables

Haiku Example: (Linda Story)

A whirr whirr of jade

Stop barely for a second

Grab nectar then go

4. *Limerick*

Five line funny poem

Lines 1, 2, and 5 rhyme

Lines 3 and 4 rhyme and are shorter

Line 5 refers to line 1

Limerick Example: *The Pelican* by Dixon Lanier Merritt (public domain)

A wonderful bird is the pelican,

His bill will hold more than his belican,

He can take in his beak

Enough food for a week

But I don't see how the helican!

Cinquain: An unrhymed five line poem

> 1 Noun
>
> 2 Adjectives
>
> 3 Present participles or verbs
>
> Short sentence about topic
>
> Synonym

Cinquain: Example by Linda Story

> Cat,
>
> Orange, black
>
> Prowling, crouching, pouncing
>
> Gazelle is on the menu
>
> Tiger

Diamante Poem: A poem of seven lines using a set structure so that the poem, when completed is in the shape of a diamond.

> Line 1: subject
>
> Line 2: two adjectives about line 1
>
> Line 3: three participles about line 1
>
> Line 4: a participial phrase about line 1, a participial phrase about line 7
>
> Line 5: three participles about line 7
>
> Line 6: two adjectives about line 7Line 7: end subject

Diamante Example: *Coal* by Linda Story

> Coal
>
> Shiny, black
>
> Resting, compressing, waiting
>
> Anticipating rebirth, arriving unchanged
>
> Cutting, grinding, polishing
>
> Shiny, white
>
> Diamond

Shape Poem or Concrete Poem: The words are written in the shape of the object the poem describes.

"The Mouse's Tale" by Lewis Carroll (public domain)

The Mouse's Tale

"FURY said to
a mouse, That
he met in the
house, 'Let
us both go
to law: *I*
will prose-
cute *you.* —
Come, I'll
take no de-
nial: We
must have
the trial;
For really
this morn-
ing I've
nothing
to do.'
Said the
mouse to
the cur,
'Such a
trial, dear
sir, With
no jury
or judge,
would
be wast-
ing our
breath.'
'I'll be
judge,
I'll be
jury,'
said
cun-
ning
old
Fury;
'I'll
try
the
whole
cause
and
con-
demn
you to
death.'

Chapter 10

Picture Books

Alignments

▶ International Literacy Association: Standard 1
▶ InTASC, Standards: 2f, 2k, 4f, 4.l, 4.q, 5h
▶ ETS, Praxis Exam: 5002 b *Test Specifications*,
▶ NCTE/CAEP: Standards 1.1, 2.2

Framework

"If you don't know what a Gryphon is, look at the picture," from *Alice's Adventures in Wonderland*

It is generally acknowledged that the most important determinant of whether children become good readers is that they are read to early and often. Parents who want their children to become good readers should read to them consistently and maximize the number of books available to them. We also know that growing vocabulary in children enhances their reading ability because children with larger passive vocabularies have greater comprehension of words when they later encounter them in print and subsequently learn to read them. Reading to children familiarizes them with the language of books and helps them to develop vocabulary and a sense of reading enjoyment.

Picture books rely equally on pictures and text to convey meaning; although, some picture books rely even more heavily on the pictures themselves than the text. Children glean meaning from the pictures, which are works of art, as well as the text. Sometimes, pictures actually provide information that the author intentionally omits from the text, allowing children to speculate and to recognize techniques such as foreshadowing. There are even examples of picture books that contain pictures that depict a story line that runs contrary to the text.

Picture books come in most of the genres described in Chapter 7. These include wordless books or first books, toy books, alphabet books, counting books, and concept books. By far, the largest genre is storybooks. Books that contain only occasional illustrations are illustrated books, not picture books.

Why and How to Use Picture Books?

Piaget's theory of cognitive development, explored in Chapter 1, holds that children learn more through their senses than adults. Indeed, children may be more attuned to the five senses than are adults, so picture books are a natural fit with children. Picture books lend themselves to engaging students, particularly when read aloud.

Three great ways to use picture books in the elementary classroom are (1) for the pure pleasure of the books, (2) to teach reading skills, and (3) to enhance content instruction. Each year, new children's books are added to the vast repertoire available in libraries and in the marketplace. In fact, the sheer numbers of books can add to the problem of selecting books for classroom use. Fortunately, in the age of communication, there are also numerous resources available to assist teachers in selecting books, several of which will be provided at the end of this chapter.

There are many ways to use picture books to enhance reading enjoyment in the classroom, even with older elementary students. Never underestimate the power of spurring a child's interest in books. It will have lifelong effect. As has been alluded to earlier, almost everyone appreciates bright colors and beautiful illustrations. The purpose for the use the book will have a bearing on how teachers introduce it, but be sure that, if reading the book aloud and showing the pictures simultaneously, all children can see. Probably the best way to do this is to sit on the floor, as most teachers do. It helps to have the children sit close, not necessarily in a circle, with the taller children in the back. This is particularly effective in the early elementary grades.

Picture books lend themselves well to grouping and learning centers because different books can be selected for different ability groupings as well as for different subjects in learning centers. Book groups or book circles with a template supplied by the teacher for a "book review" at the conclusion of the group book activity is one suggestion for keeping students on task and engaged. There are numerous ways to do this, depending upon the grade level and what we want the focus of the review to be. What follows is a possible template.

BOOK REVIEW TEMPLATE		
GROUP:		
DATE:		
TITLE:	AUTHOR:	ILLUSTRATOR:
CHARACTERS: List the main characters in the story:	CHARACTER TYPE: Describe the main character: Is the main character round, flat, dynamic, static, stock, or some other type or combination?	ILLUSTRATIONS: How did the illustrations add to the story? Give specific examples:
PLOT: List five major events in the story. Include the Climax.	THEME: What is the overall message of the story?	LITERARY DEVICES: Identify two examples of figurative language in the story.

Picture books are excellent for sustained, silent reading. We know from research that sustained silent reading is highly correlated to reading comprehension and all other literacy skills (Karshen). It is also known that instruction should follow children's interests; therefore, it is important that teachers get to know their students' interests early on so that the appropriate picture books can be in stock in the classroom. If children are interested in the books, they are more likely to stay engaged during silent reading. Another way to ensure engagement is to require a product such as an index card with two or three interesting facts or events from the reading at the conclusion of the daily silent reading period.

Picture books are excellent for **repeated reading**—having children read the same books repeatedly until they can read them fluently. Sometimes this is done by having the teacher read the book to the student first and then having the child reread until the fluency level is reached. If done aloud, this assists children in verbal skills as well as helping them become more fluent in expression and articulation. It also assists children in learning new words and increases comprehension. Think about it: When we really want to study or learn a textbook concept, don't we tend to read and reread until we know it?

Retelling: Simply asking students to retell the story from the book. Teachers can guide students as they retell by asking probing questions that relate to the evidence in the book for various segments of the retell. Comprehension can also be increased by having several students retell the same story to the class.

Reader's Theatre: Activities that involve students repeatedly reading picture books with expression. It is an activity that focuses solely on the reading itself, not on costumes or props.

Word Wall: Placing new vocabulary words that will appear in upcoming or current reading or words that are used repeatedly on a poster, smartboard, whiteboard, or other location in the classroom.

Technology: With technology in almost every classroom, teachers are able to use devices to show pictures and texts to the entire class. Children tend to love technology, and using it can keep them engaged, if used correctly.

A Word about Ideology in Picture (and other) Books

Children's literature is loaded with the ideology of the writer, the illustrator, and the social norms and values of the time. Each of us, if we are to be ethical and moral teachers, must examine the books that we choose and consider the ideologies represented in them. The following are a few questions that will help in this selection:

What is the ideology or worldview presented in this book?

- ◆ What is the political objective of this book?
- ◆ Is this an agenda that the teacher feels comfortable promoting through the use of this book in class?
- ◆ Is the subject or topic appropriate for the age and grade level of the class?
- ◆ Does this book denigrate a culture or ethnicity?
- ◆ Is this book factually and/or historically accurate? (Check the facts if uncertain)

Consider the following scenario as an example of the necessity of verifying the truthfulness and authenticity of what we teach.

Below is a speech that was published in an anthology of American Literature that the author once used in a 9th grade classroom. The speech is attributed to Sealth, Chief of the Lushootseed, Seattle Tribe. The speech was given at the occasion of the concession of Native American lands to the settlers in 1854 Washington.

> A few more moons, a few more winters, and not one of the descendants of the mighty hosts that once moved over this broad land or lived in happy homes, protected by the Great Spirit, will remain to mourn over the graves of a people once more powerful and hopeful than yours. But why should I mourn at the untimely fate of my people? Tribe follows tribe, and nation follows nation, like the waves of the sea. It is the order of nature, and regret is useless. Your time of decay may be distant, but it will surely come, for even the White Man whose God walked and talked with him as friend to friend, cannot be exempt from the common destiny. We may be brothers after all. We will see.

> We will ponder your proposition and when we decide we will let you know. But should we accept it, I here and now make this condition that we will not be denied the privilege without molestation of visiting at any time the tombs of our ancestors, friends, and children. Every part of this soil is sacred in the estimation of my people. Every hillside, every valley, every plain and grove, has been hallowed by some sad or happy event in days long vanished. Even the rocks, which seem to be dumb and dead as they swelter in the sun along the silent shore, thrill with

memories of stirring events connected with the lives of my people, and the very dust upon which you now stand responds more lovingly to their footsteps than yours, because it is rich with the blood of our ancestors, and our bare feet are conscious of the sympathetic touch. Our departed braves, fond mothers, glad, happy hearted maidens, and even the little children who lived here and rejoiced here for a brief season, will love these somber solitudes and at eventide they greet shadowy returning spirits. And when the last Red Man shall have perished, and the memory of my tribe shall have become a myth among the White Men, these shores will swarm with the invisible dead of my tribe, and when your children's children think themselves alone in the field, the store, the shop, upon the highway, or in the silence of the pathless woods, they will not be alone. In all the earth there is no place dedicated to solitude. At night when the streets of your cities and villages are silent and you think them deserted, they will throng with the returning hosts that once filled them and still love this beautiful land. The White Man will never be alone. Let him be just and deal kindly with my people, for the dead are not powerless. Dead, did I say? There is no death, only a change of worlds.

This stirring speech pays homage to the beauty and sacredness of the land. It is full of beautiful and figurative language. It laments the abuse of the land by the white settlers and decries the tragic reduction in the native population, while that of the whites increased. It has a beautiful, ethereal tone when predicting that the spirits of the Native Americans will walk the land at night when the white man thinks he is alone, and finally, it is prophetic in its prediction of the white man's eventual destiny. There is only one problem with having taught this speech: It is almost surely not authentic. Considerable study in later years revealed that Chief Seattle did not speak English. The entire speech was given in Lushootseed. There was no transcript taken of the speech; rather, the speech was actually written thirty-two years later by Dr. Henry A. Smith from his "recollection." While the fact that its authenticity is in question does not diminish the beauty or sentiment of the words, it was taught as truth, and that it was not. The moral of this story is that we are negligent if we do not examine that which we teach.

Other Considerations in Selecting Books for the Classroom

1. Choose books that are at the appropriate developmental level of the child, keeping in mind the child's current vocabulary level. If a book is too far above a child's vocabulary, he or she is likely not to enjoy the book, but books should contain a few new words and ideas. This can be tough because children in any given classroom will be at various reading levels, so it will be necessary to strike a balance.

2. Choose books that have well-developed structural elements of literature (primarily plot, characters, theme, setting, and style) covered in Chapter 4.

3. Remember that the illustrations are equally important as the story, if not more so, so choose books that contain quality illustrations that are appealing to the eye.

4. Balance selection of picture books read primarily for the story with those whose content is also valuable for instruction across the curriculum. For example, choose books that can stimulate a child's interest in content areas such as math, science, art, music, and social studies. Often a picture book is a great way to introduce a unit of study.

5. Choose books from a variety of formats including e-books to keep children interested.

Free Online Resources That Can Be Used with Picture Books

http://www.storylineonline.net/ This is a free website provided by the Screen Actors Guild. It contains videos of many picture books that are read by Hollywood actors and other celebrities. Children will recognize some of their favorite books and actors when they view the videos. Outstanding teaching activities and plans aligned with standards are also included on this site. Teachers can use this site for large group viewing or in centers.

http://en.childrenslibrary.org/ This is a free website provided by the ICDL, International Children's Digital Library. The mission of the website is to promote tolerance and respect for diverse cultures by providing access to the best of children's literature around the world. It is excellent for highlighting cultural diversity in the classroom. The website allows teachers to choose a language and to read books in that language. It contains featured books as well as award-winning books, and although it contains several reading levels and types of books, it contains many picture books. It is a little more complicated than story line online, but once one has successfully navigated it, there should be no further problems.

https://www.oxfordowl.co.uk/welcome-back/for-home The Oxford Owl is a free website provided by Oxford University Press. It consists of electronic picture books, games, and activities, but it doesn't stop there. It contains phonics, math, and other activities and tips. This site contains a wealth of free useful tools. It requires registration.

http://www.read.gov/books/ This site is provided by the Library of Congress and contains free e-book versions of classic books, mostly for children. Children can see and read the original classic versions of picture books like *Complete Version of ye three blind Mice*, *Humpty Dumpty*, and *Peter Rabbit*, many with stunning illustrations. Because the e-books contained on the site are of various reading and content levels, this is not a website that teachers should allow students to navigate on their own, but should select books for the children.

Chapter 11

Informational Books

Alignments

▶ International Literacy Association: Standard 1
▶ InTASC, Standards: 4a, 4f, 4g, 4h
▶ ETS, Praxis Exam: 5002 b *Test Specifications*,
▶ NCTE/CAEP: Standards 1.1, 1.2, 2.1, 2.2, 3.4
▶ Common Core Standards for Literacy and Next Generation Science Standards

Framework

After the original common core initiative, forty-six states adopted the common core standards. The adoption of these standards became quite controversial, and in recent years, ten of the original forty-six states have announced major changes or rewrites. Nevertheless, many of the original core standards are retained in most states (Education Week). **Common Core State Standards include literary nonfiction, expository, persuasive, and procedural as types of informational texts**.

One focus of common core standards is that of including informational texts in reading instruction. When we think about it, that makes sense. A criticism of P–12 education in the United States has long been that there is too much division and not enough integration in the teaching of skills and content. Believe it or not, there was a time during the 1990s when teachers bragged that they did not use texts. We have heard teachers brag that all activities in their classrooms were teacher created and "hands-on." There was once great criticism of teachers who relied too heavily on texts, and the result, in some cases, was that teachers did not want to use them at all or used them very little. The reader may have noted, either in this text or in personal experience that the world of education is prone to bandwagon cycles and approaches. That is why it is so important that teachers do their research and not necessarily believe that methods and approaches are research based unless the research has been validated.

We have already discussed how content knowledge actually increases reading competencies because content learned becomes known vocabulary. Content knowledge gives students a head start in reading comprehension by providing them with a prior understanding of concepts, skills, and ideas when they encounter related words in text. There are certainly thousands of instructional books available for children.

In a recent interview conducted for *Publisher's Weekly*, by Judith Rosen, July 2015, Shanta Newlin, Executive Director of Publicity at Penguin Young Readers Group stated, "We are seeing a huge lift in non-fiction sales." Newlin further indicated that sales of the top 200 titles in Penguin's nonfiction department increased by 38% in 2014.

Types of Informational Books

Informational books are just what the name implies. They provide information to children. They cover everything from arts and sciences to biographies to how to books, and they can take many forms such as textbooks, trade books, articles, e-books, and others. In order to be classified as informational, the books must consist of **provable, factual** material about any subject in the known or natural world. Children often enjoy informational books if the topics interest them. Informational books are the largest single genre in children's literature. The American Library Services for Children (ALSC) awards the Robert F. Sibert Informational Book Award each year to the author and illustrator of the most distinguished informational book for children published in English.

Types

Informational books have come a long way. At one time, they were considered boring by many, and few children read them by choice. Today, informational books can be found in all genres from picture books to texts. They are excellent teaching tools.

Elements of Informational Texts

Structure (essentially, the format that the author chooses or how the author designs the content of the book)

Theme (the point)

Style (diction, word choice, complexity of language and sentences, inclusion of tables, charts, and illustrations, etc.)

Forms of Informational Texts

Activity Books

Textbooks

Informational Chapter Books

Informational Picture Books

Concept Science or Social Studies Books

Photo Essays

Fact or List Books (almanacs, dictionaries, etc.)

Journals and Interviews

Choosing Informational Books

The selection of informational books for the classroom presents a unique problem in that the accuracy of the information must be verifiable. These are not books that children will be reading only for fun, they are meant to teach content. What is important when choosing informational books for children? First, consider whether the topic is consistent with the curriculum goals for the school and grade level. That which we teach should always be tied to the learning standards of a state or local curriculum.

Next, verify the accuracy of the information contained in the book. Who is the author and what do we know about him or her? If there is an agenda, recognize it and decide accordingly as to the value of the book for use in the classroom. A cursory look at the list of award-winning children's books through the years verifies that the books have been heavily laden with social agendas since their inception. Consider the *Orbis* book of 1648, mentioned in Chapter 2. The agenda for the book, in part, was to teach children respect for and obedience to their elders because that was part of the social agenda of the time. Today, the social agenda is different and encompasses a number of complex and controversial topics. The existence of an agenda does not necessarily rule out a book for classroom use, but it is a consideration. The important thing is that the teacher should take a neutral stance when using an agenda-driven book, and should encourage children to think critically about topics. Students need to acquire the skills of evaluating sources and evidence and forming their own opinions; in fact, those are among the common core standards.

Third, evaluate the structure of the book for clarity and user friendliness. Is the material clearly organized in such a way that it is understandable to children? Does the structure include highlights of critical concepts and information? Does the author provide illustrations that enhance meaning and will interest children?

Fourth, consider the reading level. A typical classroom is made up of children of various reading levels. Materials should be provided that address the needs of children at various levels.

Consider the following scenario in evaluating an informational picture book:

1. A teacher is considering a children's picture book about a fish who is trying to survive while somehow finding himself living in the giant trash pile that is currently floating in the Pacific Ocean.

2. The teacher determines that the content of the book is consistent with the Common Core Literacy Standards (Reading Informational Text) as well as for the Next Generation Science Standards for his grade level and will invite exploration and evaluation of the topic, presuming the information contained is accurate.

3. The teacher researches the author and finds that she has written a number of children's books that deal with the state of the environment. The likely agenda for this book is to make children aware of the problem of trash in our oceans and to evoke empathy for the wildlife living there.

4. The teacher then considers whether the information in the book is factual and determines that there is indeed a giant pile of trash floating in the Pacific Ocean and that its existence has been documented by scientists as detrimental to fish and other aquatic animals who find themselves entangled in it.

5. The teacher determines that, while environmentalism may the subject of political controversy, the information in the book is accurate as well as documented.

6. The teacher then evaluates structural elements of the text as well as the illustrations and the reading level and finds these components to be appropriate to the class.

7. The teacher determines that the book is appropriate for classroom use.

Concepts about Print and Parts of a Book

Because teachers have worked with books of all sorts for so many years, they may forget that some children enter school with little to no familiarity as to the parts of a book or how to effectively use a book. This skill is often referred to as **concepts about print** and in the early preschool years includes things like left to right orientation and page progression. In the later grades, these skills are particularly important when it comes to informational books. Although the components and their uses are simple and may appear self-evident, we cannot assume that all children know them or will discover them on their own. In Chapter 5, we talked about **qualitative elements** of books. Those are the elements that have to do with visuals, pictures, and vocabulary choice. **Quantitative elements** pertain to things that can be numbered in some sense; for example, length and complexity of sentences and structures. It is important to consider both categories in the selection of informational books, particularly since quantitative considerations can affect the child's understanding of the content.

The following are components of many informational books along with some suggestions as to how teachers can enhance student learning by ensuring that students know how to use them. Not all are found in all books.

1. Front cover: Teach students how to examine a cover of a new book for important information such as the title, the author, visual elements that are representative of the theme or content, subtitle, or tagline.

2. Back cover: Teach students how to look for information on the back cover which may include information about the author, a book summary, endorsements, etc.

3. Spine: Teach young students to be careful with the spine of a book. Show them how it holds the book together and should not be mistreated. Books of 130 pages or more typically have the following information on the spine: main title and author's last name. This aids students in locating books in a resource center.

4. Binding types: Hardcover (will have a book cover) or softcover (sometimes called dust jackets)

5. Copyright page: Title, author's name, copyright date, country where book was printed, the ISBN (International Standard Book Number), the Library of Congress number, publisher, and location where the book was printed. Teach students that they can identify the age or edition of a book from this page, so that they know if the information contained in the book is current. Students should also know that the ISBN is just an identifier that helps publishers, booksellers, libraries and others to track sales, use, and ordering.

6. Foreword: Sometimes included in nonfiction books. It is usually a description or endorsement of the book written by someone other than the author.

7. Preface: Information provided by the author, typically indicating why the book was written.

8. Introduction: Provided by the author and generally describes the book and how to use it.

9. Table of contents: The first really usable information for the student. A list of elements of the book, including those previously listed here as well as the topics, and subtopics. It provides the page numbers for each element. Teach students to look at the table of contents in order to determine where to locate information.

10. Chapters and text: The subject matter which has been identified in the table of contents.

11. Headings: Indicate topics and help guide students in their reading. They are usually in bold or colored font. Teach students to use the bold or colored type as a framework or outline to guide them in understanding and summarizing important information.

12. Captions: Located near pictures or graphics. They help to explain the pictures or graphics.

13. Diagrams, charts, graphs, maps, tables, and other images: Help to illustrate or more fully explain information that has been provided in the text.

14. Glossary: A section in the back of the book containing new or difficult terms and their definitions in alphabetical order. Students often do not even know that this element is present in a book. They should be taught to use it.

15. Index: An alphabetical listing in the back of the book containing subjects or information contained in the book and the page numbers on which the information can be found. It is much more detailed than the table of contents. Teach students to use the index if they know the terms or synonyms of the terms they are seeking. Again, many students will not notice that the book contains this feature unless the teacher points it out.

16. Appendices: Not always present in books for younger children. A section that contains additional information about topics covered in the book.

17. Bibliography: An alphabetical listing of the sources used in the writing of the book.

Chapter 12

Controversies, Challenges and Censorship

Thinking Critically about Selecting Children's Books

Arguably, one of the most prestigious awards for children's books is the Newbery Medal. Receiving this medal can launch or propel a writer's career. "A Newbery Medal can change the sales figures of a title overnight, sending books into multiple printings. Relatively few authors have ever won it, even fewer have ever won twice since the award's creation in 1922" (Barack). The award is made by a committee of fifteen members selected by the Association for Library Service to Children, a division of the American Library Association (ALA). Eight of the members are elected by members of the American Library Services for Children (ALSC) and seven are appointed by the president of the ALSC "to ensure diversity of experience and background" (Barack).

Criteria for Determining Award Winners

The ALSC describes the criteria to be considered by Newbery committee members. The following list of criteria is quoted directly from the ALSC website. In identifying "distinguished contribution to American literature," defined as text, in a book for children, the committee members should consider:

- Interpretation of the theme or concept
- Presentation of information including accuracy, clarity, and organization
- Development of a plot

- ◆ Delineation of characters
- ◆ Delineation of a setting
- ◆ Appropriateness of style (ALA)

As a teacher who makes decisions about which books are to be used, should we assume that every Newbery winner is suitable for use in our classrooms? Probably not. There are multiple criteria to consider. For example, many school systems do not allow teachers carte blanche in selecting books. Some systems, for example, require that teachers submit proposed reading lists to a committee which either approves or rejects the selections. This is true of textbooks as well. Guidelines for helping teachers select classroom books and reading lists appear in other chapters, but on the topic of choosing award winning books, the issue of the selection process is worth considering, because it is widely accepted that all award winning books for children and young adults ought to be included in the canons of school libraries. So, how does the award process work? Each year, the selection committee for the Newbery Medal, for example, is comprised of fifteen human beings, who like all other human beings, have educational, social, and political values.

The ALSC announces and publishes a list of award selection committee members each year on its website. A simple web search of the names of the committee members for any given year can give us information as to their current employment or the libraries with which they are affiliated. We may also find posts, articles, and blogs by committee members which will allow us to see the issues in which they are interested and involved. Reviewing this information can provide insight into possible agendas and/or biases, including our own. Indeed, the ALSC itself addresses the issue of bias awareness in its *John Newbery Award Committee Manual,* on page 23. "Every committee member brings unique strengths to the table, but every committee member also brings gaps in knowledge and understanding, and biases. Committee members are strongly encouraged to be open to listening and learning as well as sharing as they consider materials representing diverse experiences both familiar and unfamiliar to them." Likewise, on the same page, the ALSC affirms the value of inclusion and recognizing titles that reflect the diversity of the nation and the world" (ALSC).

After the yearly announcement of the Newbery and other winners, the inevitable controversies appear on the web. There will be those who don't like a word or words used in a particular book. For example, in 2007, Susan Patron's book, *The Higher Power of Lucky*, set off a controversy because the word "scrotum" appeared on the first page (Bosman). Other critics my note that a book contains racial or gender stereotypes, lacks diversity, or is too sexually explicit. Still others will criticize the readability or the quality.

Good teachers do their research and make informed judgments. In fact, we are charged with doing just that. Consider the following Interstate Teacher Assessment and Support Consortium (InTASC) standards: Standard 4f: "The candidate evaluates and modifies instructional resources and curriculum materials for their comprehensiveness, accuracy for representing particular concepts in the discipline, and appropriateness for his/her learners." Another relevant standard is 5k: "The candidate understands the demands of accessing and managing information as well as how to evaluate issues of ethics and quality related to information and its use." And finally, Standard 9i requires that: "The candidate understands how personal identity, worldview, and prior experience affect perceptions and expectations, and recognizes how they may bias behaviors and interactions with others" (InTASC). All this is to say that all elements of curriculum deserve careful consideration and evaluation.

Banned and Challenged Books

A movement (for lack of a better term) has grown up around the issue of making banned or challenged books available to students. The ALA sponsors a "Banned Books Week" each year during September. The ALA describes the event as follows: "Banned Books Week brings together the entire book community—librarians, booksellers, publishers, journalists, teachers, and readers of all types—in shared support of the freedom to seek and to express ideas, even those some consider unorthodox or unpopular," (ALA) in other words, in opposition to censorship.

A subsidiary of the ALA is the OIF, or Office of Intellectual Freedom, which each year publishes a list of challenged or banned books. Challenged books are those for which an attempt at removal has been made, and banned books have been removed from particular venues. To be sure, the ALA's lists of banned and challenged books are informative. Books challenged or banned virtually anywhere in the world are described. The list also provides a brief synopsis of the reasons that the books were challenged or banned. For example: the OIF notes that in a state run bookstore in Shanghai, China, *Merriam-Webster's College Dictionary* was altered in that two pages containing references to Taiwan were removed from each copy. In India, the Madras High Court refused to ban Morgan, Perumal's *One Part Woman,* which had been challenged because it depicted a formerly practiced fertility ceremony. The court's response was "If you do not like a book, simply close it. The answer is not its ban." Finally banned book in Ireland, for twelve years under Ireland's Censorship of Publications Act, was Jean Martin's *The Raped Little Runaway* for obscenity and descriptions of child rape (ALA).

The ALA/OIF website includes a case description of the books on the challenged list, so that the information is readily available to the public. Upon our review, it was found that a challenged book may have been challenged in one or more schools, school systems, or public libraries. If the challenge was successful, and many are not, the book may have been removed (banned) from reading lists, classroom assignments, or inclusion in a school or public library. In other words, the books in question are typically removed from only those venues and are not banned in the full and political sense of the word, meaning they are probably available to readers in bookstores, in other libraries, and online. The following is the list of the ALA's top ten most banned books of 2017 and the topics given on the website as to why they were banned.

1. *Thirteen Reasons Why* written by Jay Asher—suicide

2. *The Absolutely True Diary of a Part-Time Indian* written by Sherman Alexie—poverty, alcoholism, profanity, and sexual content

3. *Drama* written and illustrated by Raina Telgemeier—LGBT characters

4. *The Kite Runner* written by Khaled Hosseini—sexual violence, Islam

5. *George* written by Alex Gino—transgender child

6. *Sex is a Funny Word* written by Cory Silverberg and illustrated by Fiona Smyth—sex education

7. *To Kill a Mockingbird* written by Harper Lee—racial slurs

8. *The Hate U Give* written by Angie Thomas—drug use, profanity

9. *And Tango Makes Three* written by Peter Parnell and Justin Richardson and illustrated by Henry Cole—same sex relationship

10. *I Am Jazz* written by Jessica Herthel and Jazz Jennings and illustrated by Shelagh McNicholas—gender identity

Again, there are different interpretations of the words "banned" and "challenged." Some equate the choice of not selecting a book for a classroom or a school library with banning, particularly if the book has won an award. Others argue that choosing not to select does not mean that a book has been banned. We can probably all agree that however we choose to define the terms, choosing not to select, banning, and challenging are all forms of censorship. There are those who argue that censorship in any form is wrong, while others argue that some degree of censorship in what is provided to children for reading is appropriate. That is why it is important for teachers to make careful selections, check the local school system policies, and, it goes without saying, **never** select or recommend a book for the classroom that he or she has not read.

The National Council of Teachers of English has issued a document entitled *Guideline for Defining and Defending Instructional Methods*. In it, the Council provides advice to teachers for defending the use of books that contain profanity or racial slurs. The primary defense for including books of this nature in the canon is that it can be useful to talk about such language because students can be asked to evaluate their reaction when they first read the words in text. Students can also be asked to evaluate whether the author has used the language for the purpose of sensationalism or as a realistic representation of the way the characters in the story would talk. The Council also suggests that teachers need not read the words aloud nor have the students read them aloud (NCTE).

To be sure, there is controversy in the selection of reading materials for students, and historically, this has always been the case. Awareness of policies and possible issues can help teachers make good choices.

Further Reading on this Topic

Former Newbery chair Ellen Fader offers insider tips in her 1 August 1999, School Library Journal article, "If You Only Knew."

Jim Trelease. *Censors and Children's Lit*. www.trelease-on-reading.com/censor_entry.html

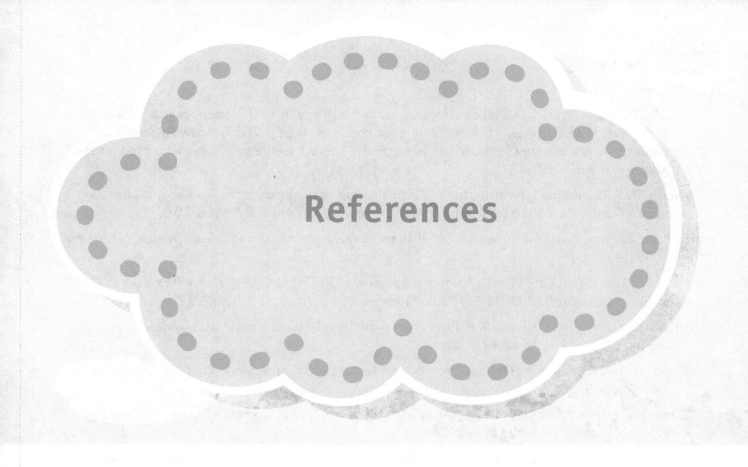

References

American Bar Association' Journal. *ABA Journal*, Aug. 1996, p. 87, www.abajournal.com/. Accessed 12 May 2017.

American Indian Library Association. *American Indian Youth Literature Award*. www.ailanet.org/activities/american-indian-youth-literature-award. Accessed 30 Apr. 2018.

American Library Association. www.ala.org/aboutala/. Accessed 14 May 2018.

American Library Association. Awards. *Newbery Medal Terms and Criteria*. www.ala.org/alsc/awards-grants/bookmedia/newberymedal/newberyterms/newberyterms/. Accessed 25 May 2018.

American Library Services for Children. ALSC. www.ala.org/alsc/. Accessed 3 June 2018.

Arbuthnot, May Hill. *Children and Books*. Scott Foresman, 1947, p. 34.

Arnove, Anthony, editor. *The Essential Chomsky*. by Noam Chomsky, vol. 1, The New Press, 2008, pp. 442-447.

ASCD. The Stages of Second Language Acquisition. www.ascd.org/publications/books/108052/chapters/The-Stages-of-Second-Language-Acquisition.aspx/. Accessed 8 May 2018.

Association of Jewish Libraries. www.jewishlibraries.org/content.php?page=Sydney_Taylor_Book_Award

Barack, Lauren. "After a Member's Ouster from Newbery Medal Committee, a Closer Look at Social Media Rules," *School Library Journal*, 6 Sept., 2017, www.slj.com/2017/09/industry-news/members-ouster-newbery-medal-committee-closer-look-social-media-rules/. Accessed 6 June 2018.

Bishop, R. S. "Selecting Literature for a Multicultural Curriculum." *Using Multiethnic Literature in the k-8 Classroom,* edited by V. J. Harris, Christopher-Gordon, 1997, pp. 1-20.

Bochner, Sandra, and Jane Jones. *Child Language Development: Learning to Talk*. Whurr Publishers, 2005.

Bosman, Julie "With One Word, Children's Book Sets Off Uproar." *New York Times*, 18 Feb. 2007, www.nytimes.com/2007/02/18/books/18newb.html/. *Accessed 6 June 2018.*

British Library. *Orbis Sensualium Pictus*. www.bl.uk/collection-items/orbis-sensualium-pictus-animal-tales-space. Accessed 5 June 2018.

Byington, Teresa, and Kim Yaebin. "Promoting Pre-Schoolers' Emergent Writing." *Young Children,* Vol. 72, no. 5, 2017.

Carnegie Greenway foundation. *The Cilip Kate Greenaway Medal*. www.carnegiegreenaway.org.uk/greenaway.php/. Accessed 5 May 2018.

Clay, M. M. "Emergent Reading Behavior." Diss., *Sage Journals*, 1966. www.journals.sagepub.com/doi/10.1177/002246697701100208/. Accessed 6 June, 2018.

Consortium of Latin American Studies. Americas Award. www.claspprograms.org/americasaward (book award)/. Accessed 6 June 2018.

Cooter, R. B., and D. R. Reutzel. *Teaching Children to Read: Putting the Pieces Together*. Pearson Education. 2004.

Corbett, Sue, "New Trends in YA, the Agent's Perspective." *Publisher's Weekly,* 27 Sept. 2013, www.publishersweekly.com/pw/by-topic/childrens/childrens-industry-news/article/59297-new-trends-in-ya-the-agents-perspective.html/. Accessed 30 May 2018.

Craig, Amanda. "Why This Is a Golden Age for Children's Literature, Children's Books Are One of the Most Important Forms of Writing We Have. Speech, www.independent.co.uk/arts-entertainment/books/features/why-this-is-a-golden-age-for-childrens-literature-childrens-books-are-one-of-the-most-important-10340568.html/. Accessed 28 May, 2018.

Education Week. *Common Core States*. www.edweek.org/ew/section/multimedia/map-states-academic-standards-common-core-or.html/. Accessed 30 Apr. 2018.

Educational Testing Service. *Elementary Education: Multiple Subjects. Elementary Education: Multiple Subjects*. Educational Testing Service. 2017.

Eisenstein, Elizabeth. *The Printing Press as an Agent of Change: Communication and Cultural Transformation in Early Modern Europe*. vol. 2, Cambridge UP. 1980, pp. 43-88.

Fagan, Brian, and Charlotte Beck, editors. *The Oxford Companion to Archeology*. Oxford UP, 1966.

Fischer-Wright, Blanch. *Arbuthnot, May Hill, Introduction to the Real Mother Goose, Special Anniversary Edition*. Chicago: Rand McNally, 1965.

Frith, U. "Beneath the Surface of Developmental Dyslexia," *Surface Dyslexia, Neuropsychological and Cognitive Studies of Phonological Reading*, edited by K. Patterson, J. Marshall, and M. Coltheart, Erlbaum, London, 1985, pp. 301-330.

Gabriel, Trip.. "Oh Jane, See How Popular We Are." *New York Times*, 1996, https://www.nytimes.com/1996/10/03/garden/oh-jane-see-how-popular-we-are/. Accessed 10 May 2018.

Graves, Donald H. "Writing: Teachers and Children at Work," *In Emerging Literacy: Young Children Learn to Read and Write*, edited by, D. S. Strickland and L. M. Morrow. International Reading Association Newark. Del, 1989.

Gruner, E. R. "Education," *Keywords for Children's Literature*, edited by P. Nell and L. Paul. New York UP, 2011, pp. 70-74.

Hallo, William, W. *The World's Oldest Literature: Studies in Sumerian Belles-Lettres*. Brill, Boston, 2010, p. 63.

Harris, T. L., and Hodges, R. E., editors. "*The Literacy Dictionary: The Vocabulary of Reading and Writing*." *International Reading Association*. 1995.

International Board on Books for Young Children. *Hans Christian Andersen Awards*. www.ibby.org/awards-activities/awards/hans-christian-andersen-awards/?L=0/. Accessed 3 May 2018.

Interstate Teacher Assessment and Support Consortium. *Model Core Teaching Standards, 2017*, Council of Chief State School Officers. www.ccsso.org/resource-library/intasc-model-core-teaching-standards/. Accessed 6 June 2018.

Jane Addams Peace Foundation (Award). www.janeaddamschildrensbookaward.org/jacba/. Accessed 6 June 2018.

"Jean-Jacques Rousseau" article in *The Basics of Philosophy* (Philosophy Basics). www.philosophybasics.com/philosophers_rousseau.html/. Accessed 1 May 2018.

Knowles, Murray, and Kirsten Malmkjaer. *Language and Control in Children's Literature, London and New York, Routledge, 1995.*

Kroll, B. M., and R. J. Vann, editors. "Developmental Relationship between Speaking and Writing Exploring Speaking-Writing Relationships: Connections and Contrasts." *National Council of Teachers of English*, 1981, pp. 32-54.

"Laura Ingalls Wilder" *Encyclopedia Britannica*. www.britannica.com/biography/Laura-Ingalls-Wilder/. Accessed 1 May 2018.

Learning Timeline, the 1400's, British Library. www.bl.uk/learning/timeline/item107718.html/. Accessed 12 May 2018.

Locke, John. "The Educational Writings of John Locke." *World Heritage Encyclopedia*, Project Gutenberg. www.central.gutenberg.org/articles/eng/John_Locke/. Accessed 5 May 2018.

Matthews, Gareth. *Philosophy & the Young Child*. Harvard UP, 1994, p. 4.

McLeod, S. "B.F. Skinner | Operant Conditioning | Simply Psychology." *Simplypsychology.org*, 2017. www.simplypsychology.org/operant-conditioning.html/. Accessed 7 Apr. 2017.

McNamara, Charles. "In the image of God; John Comenius and the First Children's Picture Book." Essay in *Public Domain Review*.www.publicdomainreview.org/2014/05/14/in-the-image-of-god-john-comenius-and-the-first-childrens'-picture-book/. Accessed 3 May 2018.

Montanaro, Ann. *A Concise History of Pop-up and Movable Books.* www.libraries.rutgers.edu/rul/libs/scua/montanar/p-intro.htm/. Accessed 3 June 2018.

National Book Foundation writers. www.nationalbook.org/aboutus_history.html#.WwMPX-T7lPY/. Accessed 5 Apr. 2018.

National Council for the Social Studies (Book award). www.socialstudies.org/. Accessed 28 Apr. 2018.

National Council of Teachers of English. www2.ncte.org/awards/orbis-pictus-award-nonfiction-for-children/. Accessed 2 June 2018.

National Council of Teachers of English. *Defining and Defending Instructional Methods,* Position Statement, 23 July 1998, www.ncte.org/positions/statements/defendinginstrmethod/. Accessed 5 May 2018.

Nel, Phillip, "Dr. Seuss, An American Icon" synopsis on Seussville, www.seussville.com/author/SeussBio/. Accessed 28 May 2018.

The New London Group. "A Pedagogy of Multi-literacies: Designing Social Futures." *Harvard Educational Review*: April, Vol. 66, No. 1, 1996, pp. 60-93, www.hepgjournals.org/doi/10.17763/haer.66.1.17370n67v22j160u?code=hepg-site/. Accessed 18 May 2018.

Payne, Lynda. "Health in England (16th-18th c.)." *Children and Youth in History,* Item #166.

PBS. *The Greeks.* www.pbs.org/empires/thegreeks/background/24c.htm. Accessed 5 May 2018.

Plimpton, George, "The Hornbook and Its Use in America." *Proceedings of the American Antiquarian Society,* vol. 26, 1916, pp. 264-72.

Royster, Paul, editor. *Milk for Babes. Drawn Out of the Breasts of Both Testaments. Chiefly, for the Spirituall Nourishment of Boston Babes in Either England: But May Be of Like Use for Any Children (1646),* [Abstract] retrieved from Digital Commons @ University of Nebraska, Lincoln, www.digitalcommons.unl.edu/etas/18/. Accessed 4 June 2018.

Schickedanz, Judith A. "Much More than the ABCs: The Early Stages of Reading and Writing." *National Association for the Education of Young Children*, 1999.

Sendak, Maurice. "Randolph Caldecott." *Caldecott & Co. Notes on Books and Pictures*, edited by Essay, New York, Noonday Press, 1988, pp. 21-50.

Sommerville, J. P. *The Early Modern Family.* University of Wisconsin, Madison, 2018. www.faculty.history.wisc.edu/sommerville/367/367-033.htm. Accessed 5 May 2018.

Sparks, Sarah D. "Study: Third Grade Reading Predicts Later High School Graduation." *Education Week.org, Education Week*, 8Apr. 2011, www.blogs.edweek.org/edweek/inside-school-research/2011/04/the_disquieting_side_effect_of.html/. Accessed 23 May 2018.

Spufford, Margaret. *Small Books and Pleasant Histories: Popular Fiction and Its Readership in Seventeenth-Century England,* Methuen, London, 1981.

Spufford, Margaret. *The Great Reclothing of Rural England,* London, The Hambeldon P, 1984.

Texas State University. *Rivera Book Award*. www.education.txstate.edu/ci/riverabookaward/

Temple, Charles, Ruth Nathan, Frances Temple, and Nancy Burris. *The Beginnings of Writing*, Section 1, New York, Pearson, 1992.

National Association for the Education of Young Children. www.naeyc.org/resources/pubs/yc/nov2017/emergent-writingUS/. Accessed 8 Apr. 2018.

US CENSUS BUREAU? *2000 US Census Bureau Web 15 Oct 2009. Accessed 1 June 2018.*

Wilfong, Lori Georgianne. "A Mirror, a Window: Assisting Teachers in Selecting Appropriate "Multicultural Young Adult Literature." ***International Journal of Multicultural Education,*** [Sl.], vol. 9, no. 1, Dec. 2007. ISSN 1934-5267. www.ijme-`journal.org/index.php/ijme/article/view/7/74. Accessed 04 June 2018.

CPSIA information can be obtained
at www.ICGtesting.com
Printed in the USA
LVHW061139010521
686096LV00001B/1